THE COMPLETE GUIDE TO

MAVERICK
PODCASTING

THE COMPLETE GUIDE TO
MAVERICK
PODCASTING

A MANUAL FOR NONCONFORMISTS

MICAH HANKS

ROCKETEER PRESS • ASHEVILLE, NORTH CAROLINA

ISBN-13: 978-0692522462

Visit www.micahhanks.com and www.maverickpodcasting.org for more information.

For Race Hobbs, a true friend and brother... hbs.

CONTENTS

THE COMPLETE GUIDE TO
MAVERICK
PODCASTING

ACKNOWLEDGEMENTS

In appreciation of those who lent inspiration to this project, and for those who have helped me with it along the way, I wish to express my sincere thanks and appreciation. Without them, not only would it be likely that this book would never have existed, but there would have hardly been any reason to write it in the first place. Through their hard work and achievement, each of these individuals has played a role in helping make the podcasting medium what it is for us today.

To Adam Curry, the godfather of podcasting, and producer of what his listeners know to be "The Best Podcast in the Universe", which he issues twice weekly with the honorable John C. Dvorak; to Cliff Ravenscraft for his innumerable contributions to the podcasting medium, for his time and hours spent educating others on how to do it themselves, and for his patience in answering my email queries during the authorship of this book; to Pat Flynn for his positive energy, and for his encouragement with this project, as well as his willingness to correspond despite schedules as busy as both of ours tend to be; to Jim Harold for his friendship, and for the brainstorming sessions we frequently share, as well as the wonderful foreword he offered for this book; to George Noory and Tom Danheiser of *Coast to Coast AM*, who have been wonderful friends to have in all this, both on and off the microphone; and finally, to John W. Anderson, the original guru of radio production who, like Yoda building a Jedi out of the youthful Luke Skywalker, helped to train me in the arts of audio wizardry at an early age, and set me on a course toward self reliance and appreciation for the art, and the music, of the human voice.

To each of you, an expression of sincere thanks is hardly enough to acknowledge the effect you've had on this project, but I offer it here nonetheless. Thank you, so very much.

FOREWORD

Podcasting changed my life, and I believe it can change yours. That is why I was delighted to help when my friend Micah Hanks asked me to write this foreword for *The Complete Guide to Maverick Podcasting*.

I began podcasting in 2005, and my how things have things changed since then! Back in those days, when I mentioned that I was a podcaster, the most common reply was, "a *whatcaster?*" Jump forward to today, as I write this at a time when nearly every comedian has their own podcast, most of the population is carrying around a Smartphone (the perfect podcast receiver), breakout podcasts like *Serial* and *WTF* are breaking into the pop culture, and even Saturday Night Live now does parodies of popular podcasts; all sure signs this medium is reaching critical mass.

According to a 2015 Edison Research study, an estimated 46 million Americans had listened to at least one podcast in the last month. That is a *lot* of people, and that number is growing every day.

Reader, as I am assuming you may be relatively new to the idea of becoming a podcaster, I have three pieces of really good news for you:

➤ While podcasting has exploded, what we're seeing now is only the beginning. If the stats I referenced above from Edison Research are correct, that means that over 250 million Americans *don't* yet listen to podcasts on a monthly basis. That also means there is HUGE potential for this medium, and it isn't too late to become a part of it... but don't wait *too long!*

➤ As podcasting becomes easier to enjoy in our cars through systems like Android Auto and Apple's Car Play, the medium will become a real challenger to talk radio, and the aforementioned numbers will only skyrocket further.

➤ Finally, in your hands you hold a book, *The Complete Guide to Maverick Podcasting*, which can walk you through the process of becoming a podcaster, and all without having to go bankrupt or insane.

For me, podcasting started as a hobby that eventually became my full time profession. I love it. With it, I have met interesting people, written best selling books, spent more time with my family than a regular nine-to-five would allow, and left a job I pretty much hated to became a "micro celebrity", all due to podcasting. Granted, I am not sitting on a huge bank account, but there is still time to work toward that, and at present, it is a very rewarding lifestyle.

I am constantly amazed when I get fan mail from the UK, Japan, Australia, and other places from all around the globe. Just think, I produce all of this content in my little home office in Ohio, and yet what began as a hobby for me can have an impact on people worldwide. We are truly living in a time when, thanks to our technology, an individual can make their voice heard in ways that even the biggest broadcasters couldn't have dreamed of twenty years ago.

For you, podcasting might not become your full time job, but I think it can accentuate pretty much any hobby or profession out there. If you are a bottle cap collector, then I bet you could create a podcast on the subject, and become well known in your community of fellow-collectors in no time. Professionally, podcasting can help you network and give you expert status in almost any field. And the good news is that there is only one person you need permission from to do it, and that's *you*.

So with that, it's time for you to dig into *The Complete Guide to Maverick Podcasting*. With this book, Micah has provided you with a roadmap, so pick it up, and begin your journey. And lastly, I hope podcasting changes your life, for the better, as much as it did mine.

Happy podcasting!

Jim Harold
August 2015

Jim Harold is a professional podcaster and has been producing programs on the paranormal since 2005. His free podcasts have been downloaded over 18 million times. You can find his podcasts at jimharold.com and his "Podcasting Without Breaking The Bank" on-demand video course at podcastwithjim.com.

INTRODUCTION

Sharing our lives with others is a fundamental part of being human. We share with those around us because we want to express some part of ourselves to the world, and because doing so can make us feel closer to one another.

For instance, when our favorite sports team brings victory on the field, we share the celebration of that victory with like-minded fans. When we reach new personal milestones in our lives, we often create posts about them to share with our friends on social media sites; and when we meet someone whose company we can't bear the thought of being without, true love can lead to a commitment where we vow to share our entire life with another person.

Sharing our lives can be a fundamental part of our existence for other reasons, too. For example, aspects of your personal life may become public when you are:

> A famous celebrity who, for good or for ill, is beleaguered by paparazzi that

follows you around like hungry vultures waiting for a struggling baby rabbit to die, cataloguing your every movement as though tomorrow, and every other day too, actually depended on it

➢ A desperate, cash-strapped nobody who's tired of living on a couch in your parent's basement, and you've suddenly gotten wise to the idea that you could make millions off of exploiting your lifestyle as a spectacle on a new reality television show

➢ A person who is running for political office or reelection who, at the advice of your campaign staff, now knows that you must parade your family and personal activities around on the campaign trail with you so potential voters will think your life was crafted from a lost archive of unaired episodes of *Leave it to Beaver*

I think you see where I'm going with this. In other words, many people today have found that they can promote what they do, how they do it, and whom they do it with, and often for more than just self-gratification. When done properly, the information you share with the world can actually bring you fame, and yes, even fortune.

Which brings us to the all-important topic that made you pick up this book in the first place: *podcasting*.

The world is changing, and with it, so is media, and the way we use it to communicate ideas. Anyone who has worked in the broadcasting industry knows, for instance, that the market for terrestrial radio stations that broadcast music was changed by the advent of listen-on-demand options, ranging from portable mp3 players, to streaming sites that offer access to music for free, just like radio does. The catch here is that listening online offers music that's not just played in random order like most top-forty stations would do. Listeners now have the option of customizing what they hear, so they can essentially create their own music stations that stream high-quality audio via the Internet, and only play songs they will actually enjoy hearing.

Many thought technology like this would be the end of radio, but that was far from being the case. The industry simply followed suit, and decided to jump on the bandwagon by crafting Smartphone apps and other tools to bring their content to listeners in new ways; but that's not to say that the new, and ever-growing number of options for consumers haven't made things at least a bit challenging for traditional radio stations.

Talk radio has experienced the same challenges, to an extent, since people who once religiously tuned in to hear their favorite pundits and shock-jocks now also have the ability to listen to shows on-demand, and to a broader variety of them, at any time they choose. Such shows can be downloaded automatically to people's phones and other portable devices at little or no cost. These are the podcasts that people like you and me listen to, and which soon you will also be creating, if you aren't doing so already.

The beauty of the podcast as a form of media is its accessibility, both to consumers, as well as producers. It is a medium once reserved only for those who could convince a radio station to give them airtime, which now grants a voice to virtually anyone with internet access that is willing to invest in the tools, and the time needed to learn how to create an audio file of their show, and make it accessible online to potential listeners. Perhaps of equal importance is that podcasting, since it *doesn't* require having to have a radio station or other facility backing it like talk programs needed in the old days, also becomes a portable medium. This is not only a benefit; being portable (and hence flexible) is a fundamental aspect of the podcasting philosophy, as well as a key element to shaping one's lifestyle, which I will emphasize throughout this book.

In the spirit of honesty, I'll say that I could go on about how podcasts are revolutionizing the way people get their news and entertainment, and toss numbers and figures at you to offer statistical proof. But I would guess that because you're reading this, you already *know* the power of the podcast, and you're probably more than ready to get a piece of the action for yourself.

Hence, I want to take a brief moment to tell you what this book is aimed at helping you do, what you'll find in it, and perhaps most important of all, what you *will not* find in this book.

There are a lot of resources available on the Internet for people who are hoping to learn how to become a podcaster, from blog posts by skilled audio wizards and tech professionals, to countless books written by expert podcasters, and even entire websites devoted to nothing but teaching and providing the tools needed for anyone to properly learn the right way to do it all (to help you find these kinds of resources, as an added bonus, I've gone about compiling a list of them for you, which you'll find in the **appendix** section in the back of this book).

With all of this material already dedicated to this subject, my goal here isn't to try and compete with those other resources, and simply regurgitate what those sites and books are already saying. There are really just three key ideas that pushed me to want to write this book for you:

> Despite the constant changes in the industry and with technology in general, a surprising number of decent books about podcasting are already several years old

> Most books and sites that teach people about podcasting deal almost entirely with the technical aspects (often even laboriously so), with little said about the "art" of creating compelling, worthy content—a BIG part of whether or not people will listen to you in the first place—and doing so on a budget when necessary

> Podcasting has had a huge influence on my lifestyle and philosophy, largely because it is an activity that you can take with you anywhere you go, and still achieve quality results (that is, as long as

you have the right tools, and a knowledge of how to use them). This has opened my mind to new possibilities about how to succeed with entrepreneurial endeavors, how to use podcasts and other media to promote things like your business, and how to obtain the freedom needed to live your life *your way*, by pursuing your passions and dreams

I might add, in fairness, that I'm only human, like the majority of you that will eventually come into possession of this book (though I do wonder why more cats aren't producing podcasts, since they tend to think they can do anything a human can, and also do it better). I'm also a self-described nonconformist, which explains why I've been self-employed for several years now, using the podcasts I produce to broaden my knowledge as a writer, as well as help promote my other entrepreneurial endeavors. I'm even able to use podcasting to generate some of the income that helps me make a living, which I'll discuss in greater depth later in this book. More often, however, I enjoy podcasting for the fun, and for its ability to help my insatiable drive to be involved in things happening in our world in a meaningful way.

Keeping the discussion going on important issues, and promoting the exchange of ideas in a responsible, intelligent way, I feel, are great ways each of us can contribute to society.

As I'm doing here, a lot of podcasters and bloggers emphasize lifestyle as part of what they focus on with their work; Pat Flynn is an excellent example of this. In addition to being one really down-to-earth, and downright inspirational fellow, he is also somebody that makes an impressive living each year, and he'll tell you about it at his website www.smartpassiveincome.com, where he features a counter at the top of the page that indicates his monthly income. But the great thing about Pat is that he's equally dedicated to helping his followers do the same thing. That's because being successful at anything is, in part, about the kind of lifestyle you want to have, and how you relate aspects of it to others. As Pat explains, he lost his day job a few years ago, and decided to try writing, podcasting, and generating what he calls *smart passive income* as an alternative to finding another "real" job; few would argue that he came out better off as a result!

Of greater importance, through the hardship presented by losing his job, Pat learned, like countless others have, that these kinds of problems also present us with new opportunities, if we're patient enough to see where the stepping stones may lead. With time, and persistence, taking that road less traveled can also lead to a kind of freedom that most people will never know.

My guess would be, however, that the majority of people are so concerned about failing along the way, that they never take that first step toward living a new kind of life to begin with. Many of us will spend the duration of our lives feeling trapped, and thinking there is nothing better out there waiting for us; we easily forget that before a mile can be traveled, we have to take that first step.

Podcasting is great to me because, as I mentioned earlier, it is a medium you can use not only to promote other things you do, but also one that can go with you anywhere the road of life may lead you. Rather than being the answer to all of your problems, I have found that it is a tool that can help you along the way, and if freedom and self-reliance are among your goals, it is certainly something that may help get you there.

But not everyone who produces a podcast is doing it to achieve financial goals, freedom, or other similar things. Coming back to the idea of involving ourselves in meaningful things, there are some podcasts that are produced as a service to the community, or maybe for discussion and preservation of things like historical and scientific knowledge. Some people are driven to create podcasts because they want to learn more about obscure subjects like unexplained phenomena in nature (as I did), and contribute to further dialogue about it. Others may feel drawn to podcasting because they find that good information on a topic they're interested in seems to lack any quality discussion in the form of similar podcasts. For every popular subject that has twenty or more podcasts devoted to it, there are probably hundreds of others that no one ever stopped to consider what interest they might generate, let alone the kind of reach they may eventually have, if only the right voice were behind them.

So at this point, I want you to stop for a moment, and ask yourself: *why do I want to create a podcast?*

It sounds like a simple question, but I often find that when I ask this of people who come to me wanting to get pointers for kicking off their own podcasts, they often don't really have an answer. It's fair to ask, since I'm always interested in hearing why anyone would want to commit themselves to the kind of thing that requires hours of work that may go unpaid for a long, *long* time, and if any kind of "thanks" is ever offered, it may be in the form of scathing criticism from your listenership.

Think about that for a minute, and tremble a little if necessary, while I get a cup of coffee. You may need one too, in fact, because this is intended to be a wakeup call.

Of course, here I'm outlining the worst-case scenario. In my own experience, nothing about podcasting has ever *really* been as bad as I may have just made it out to be. Still, my question is an important one: *why do you want to be a podcaster?* Asking this question is central to understanding a lot of things, including why I came to believe this book needed to be written.

When I began podcasting, I was already somebody who spent a lot of time on the road. I was (and am still) a musician, and I travel frequently as part of performing with a working acoustic group. I'm also a writer, but before I had published any books, there was a period after I had left my previous day job in broadcast radio, where I was exploring new ways to become self-employed, particularly by using the Internet. I had been a producer of talk shows, and would work fairly odd, and often long hours, running the board for shows that dealt with everything from politics and sports, to holistic wellness, science, and investing. Hence, it was working in radio that introduced me to the thrill of being behind a microphone; on occasion, I might even get the opportunity to sit in as a guest host on various programs when the regular hosts couldn't be there for a live shift. It wasn't long before I had the bug, and in the back of my mind, I knew that podcasting would be a viable way to quench the insatiable desire to broadcast, but without having to do it on the terms my overlords at the giant corporate radio conglomerate had demanded (*translation:* "Micah, we'll give you a half hour spot at 5 AM on Saturday mornings, if you can find sponsors to pay *us* for the airtime").

When I left radio to pursue being a writer, I hadn't really listened to very many podcasts. As it came time to begin promoting my first self-published book, a friend of mine (also a radio host, incidentally) had even told me, "don't bother going on those podcasts and internet shows, unless you're happy with just twelve people listening." He was convinced it hadn't been worth his time to do so in the past, and that it wouldn't be worth my time, either.

Fortunately, I was skeptical.

As my homespun publicity campaign began, the first interview request that I received had been from a podcast called *Mysterious Universe*, who also offered me a job blogging for them shortly afterward. All these years later, I still enjoy writing every article I contribute to their site. Additionally, when I finally decided to launch my own podcast, it was through my appearances on that program, with its tremendous following, that helped my future listenership learn about the show I was now producing. Needless to say, I'm glad I didn't take my friend's advice about limiting my participation in podcast interviews!

More central to why this book was written, as I've expressed already, is that I'm also somebody who enjoys traveling. Because of this, I realized early on that there would be a necessity for being able to have equipment that would let me take my podcasting operation on the road with me, without sacrificing the quality of the content I hoped to produce. Hence, when it came time to write this book, one of the things I felt had been lacking in other literature about podcasting was information for people who like to be able to take their podcasting production with them wherever they go.

Podcasters who can do what they do while traveling have the ability not only to take their work with them everywhere they go, but they can also document their travels, and incorporate the adventures they have into the content they produce. Think of it as sort of like being a travel writer, only you record audio about the places you visit, rather than simply writing it down.

This area of what I call the "art" behind podcasting is something that, while not entirely overlooked by other writers, is certainly less often addressed; and yet, I actually find it to be one of the most enjoyable things about being a dedicated podcaster. I should note that when I say "dedicated," I mean that a big part of what ensures your success as a podcaster relies on your dedication to maintaining a schedule of some sort: whether it be every week, or every other month, generally your listeners like to know that, eventually, they're going to hear something from you. Hence, if you travel a lot like I do, you have to be able to do your show just as easily wherever it is you're going, or maybe even on your way there, if necessary.

This book will not only address how to take your podcast with you wherever you go, but it will offer you *one of the most important keys among any other advice I could hope to give you:* **options**. Sure, as I've stumbled my way along the path to successful podcast production, I've encountered many sites and books over the years that will tell you how to do "this" or "that", and especially try to drive home a certain way that it "must be done." There are a lot of ways that qualify as the "right" way to produce a podcast; and there are also a lot of really, really wrong ways to do things that you should avoid.

In my view, this is the importance of having *options* presented for the reader, because in the past I've found myself pulling my hair out trying to figure out something my instincts told me would be easy, but which never seemed to come across as easily-done on the printed page. Nine times out of ten, I was generally right about my intuition when it came to such things, and it took me looking elsewhere to find options that would help me overcome what might have been a simple hurdle, had only the author I'd been reading known (or taken the time to find) alternatives to things like the best way to produce an RSS feed specifically for a podcast, or how to set up a payment system for a subscriber area, or how to change your podcast artwork on the sites of various podcast clients like iTunes, and literally countless numbers of other questions one will eventually find themselves asking about this subject.

Some of you may have bought this book with full knowledge of the answers to questions like those I've listed above, and hope instead to use this book as a reference, as opposed to a book that's to be read front-to-back. If so, I encourage you to jump around and read the chapters and sections that are most relevant to where you are with your own podcasting. The kinds of options I will hope to provide along the way will still be aimed at helping you get the most out of it in a way that fits your lifestyle, and in a way that helps meet your expectations for whatever it is you hope to get out of all this by becoming a podcaster in the first place.

But if you're absolutely new to this, and still wondering where exactly you should begin, I *strongly* recommend taking things from the beginning of chapter one, and read through with each subsequent chapter until the end. You'll see as we go that there is an "order of operations" that can be applied intelligently to podcasting, and if it's followed, it can help prevent a lot of problems down the road.

A book like this, aimed specifically at the kind of approach to podcasting I've been describing in this introduction, is by no means exhaustive (although there are plenty of other books on the subject which *are* exhaustive; and which, in many cases, provide a *lot* more information than the average podcaster will really ever need). Here, I will hope to address a lot of the major issues and questions I've encountered over the last few years, as a podcaster who enjoys freedom and mobility, but who also strives for quality audio production at all costs. It is my hope that teaching you some of the key principles early on may save you several headaches later, and give you insights through advice on what I would personally choose to do, based on my own experiences as a podcaster.

Granted, as I stated earlier, I'm human, and that means I'm not perfect. Therefore, you may find that there are questions you had when you bought this that I haven't addressed by the time you finish with the book; and if that's the case, don't panic and throw the book on the ground, dumping that precious cup of coffee all over it as frustration spills forth from your angry soul. Save the coffee, for goodness sake, and throw the book on the ground instead.

In fact, let it stay there for a while, as you carry your coffee over to your laptop, where you can write me an email with the question you couldn't find answers for in this book. I can be reached at info@micahhanks.com, and if I know of a solution, I'll be sure to answer your question. If I can't do it right off the top of my head, I'll try to help you find somebody that can.

See, aren't you glad you didn't pour out that coffee?

With that, we've got a lot of area to cover, so indulge yourself by knocking back another hearty helping of that caffeinated nectar, and let's get into how you can be podcasting like a dedicated nonconformist in no time, you *maverick*. Don't worry; my mom calls me that too: "maverick." It's just a thing, and I promise, you'll get used to it.

CHAPTER ONE: BEFORE YOU BEGIN

So you've made up your mind: *you're going to be a podcaster.*

Good for you. The simple decision to take action has served as the romantic ideal that launched the careers of countless successful individuals over the centuries, which knew in their hearts that they would one day do something great, regardless of whether or not they knew *how* it might be accomplished. It brings to mind a quote from American poet Carl Sandburg, often misquoted as a much earlier proverb of mysterious and ancient origins, which said, "I'm an idealist. I don't know where I'm going, but I'm on my way."

This is a healthy attitude to have, to some extent. No one, I feel, should allow the intimidation of unknown solutions to foreseeable obstacles prevent positive action from being taken. But allow me to tell you, before you get bustling too far down that road of unknowing, that in the world of podcasting it *really does* help to have at least some idea about where you're eventually headed.

For starters, even before you begin learning the technical aspects of how a podcast works, and what kinds of equipment you'll need in order to achieve the best sound possible, it is equally important to give consideration to things like **the name of your podcast**, and what it's central focus will be.

What's in a Name?

Bands change their names, as do ball teams, certain holidays, and even certain children upon reaching legal adulthood, whose parents bestowed them with eccentric, unpronounceable series of vowel sounds and clicking noises for names when they were born.

While we know that certain names just have to change from time to time, this is *not* something you will typically want to do with your podcast, and here's why: the name you will ultimately choose for the show you'll end up producing will be *the number one most important identifier people will associate with you*, next to your own name. And on that note, incorporating your *actual* name into the show's title isn't a bad idea either!

A number of famous podcasters have used this deceptively simple "I used my actual name" method of producing a title for their shows. One that comes to mind is comedian Joe Rogan, whose fine podcast *The Joe Rogan Experience* deals with a variety of alternative subjects. Any quick search for podcasts online will display similar shows that use the host's name, or some phrase that presents a variation on it, as the title of their podcast. One thing I particularly like about this method of naming is that by branding *yourself* as the focus of the show, your title will be less limiting in terms of the kinds of topics you may choose to address (and keep in mind, your interests may begin to change with time, so you'll want a name that will still reflect those kinds of changes, regardless of where you go with the subjects you choose to discuss. We'll address the topic of "changing subjects" in greater detail in a minute).

Apart from using your name in the actual title of your podcast, another approach is to feature the host's name in the subtitle instead. This is useful if your podcast would benefit from having a name that is similar to (or even identical to) the name of something else you may be promoting, like your business. Let's say you're an entrepreneur, and your ultimate goal is to promote your business online by reaching as many people as possible, using a free podcast with information about your trade. You may even want to devote time to advertising how your business and the services you provide can help listeners who need assistance in related areas.

All these things are worthy of consideration as you're coming up with ideas about what you'll call your podcast, but just to be sure we're covering all the bases, a few more practical considerations are:

➢ Whatever name you decide on, read it aloud and ask yourself, *can my listeners pronounce this?* You may feel like it's a good idea to use some exotic word or phrase, perhaps as a simple matter of style, and that's your prerogative. But I would try to avoid it, and use clear, simple words that describe what your show is about.

➢ Another wise consideration (and in truth, I should probably say it's mandatory) is to perform a search online to see if another show is already using the name you've chosen. The last thing you want is to build a decent audience over time, only to get hit with a complaint or "cease and desist" letter from somebody who had been using the name previously... and was wise enough to trademark that title.

➢ You'll also want to search online to see if a domain that uses your prospective title already exists. Domain parking can be big business if a prospective owner is willing to shell out enough money—often *thousands* of dollars or more—to secure a specific domain for their business. If you're among the young, fabulous, and broke, then depending on the title you choose, you may have to get creative with variations that include *.org*, *.info*, etc, if the .com address with your show's title is already taken.

It may not seem important at the outset to have your own web domain associated with the title of your podcast. You may even be thinking, *how am I supposed to be able to afford my own web domain?* (In fact, I would prefer you were thinking that right now, as opposed to the fantasy about the monkeys with bow ties and pound cakes again). The truth is that owning a website can be as inexpensive as just a few dollars a month; that's right, you'll spend more on a meal at the fast food place down the street than what it would cost you each month to host your own site, depending on what service you choose. Still, I'm not here to try and convince you to buy web space, or better yet, to launch your own server farm and host your site independently like the Romans would have done it. In the next chapter, we'll be looking at inexpensive options for podcasters that cost you little, or perhaps even *nothing* to host your podcast; but I'll warn you now, as you've probably heard before, *you get what you pay for.* The same principle applies here, so don't expect amazing results if you aren't at least willing to pay a little. What you'll get may suit your needs... but it will be far from being optimal.

If you're interested in getting into podcasting to promote an existing business, the often-minimal costs associated with web hosting probably aren't going to be huge concerns for you. You may even have a website for your business already (and if not, then welcome to the 21st century, Rip van Winkle. Now let's get you a haircut). Even if you weren't looking to get into podcasting for business reasons, I would argue that the same principles apply here with regard to thinking ahead. Whether or not profit is your goal, getting your content out there to people and building a following will rely on practices very similar to how a business is promoted and grown. This comes back to the question of why you want to produce a podcast in the first place; as you can see, it's helpful to at least have some sort of idea of what you want to do, and where you'll see yourself on down the road in a few months, or maybe a few years from now, before you launch.

A final few words come to mind for those of you interested in branding the name of your show, and communicating effectively to people what you and your show are about. With your show's title, or with your name, or any combination of the two, you can also add **keywords** that will help describe what your show is about. If you're a gardener whose show will emphasize organic gardening, pest control, and the best crops to grow in various climates, you might call your show something like *Practical Organic Gardening: Climate, Produce, and Protecting Your Crops*, where "Practical Organic Gardening" is the title, and *climate, produce,* and *protecting* are your branding keywords. Since most podcasting services you'll submit your show to will also want to know the title of the host or talent, you might list your name and occupation something like this: "Jezebel Bush (or whatever your name actually is): Gardener, Consultant, Organic Enthusiast."

You should consider using keywords in places like your podcast's listing in the iTunes store. Of course, these sorts of keywords may not need to be featured on every bit of artwork or other promotional material you offer with your show; for example, your iTunes artwork may just feature the words, *Practical Organic Gardening with Jezebel*

Bush. But using keywords in situations where actual text is involved will improve search engine results, helping you to reach a broader range of people that may find your subject interesting. We'll talk more specifically about how and where these elements can be added later on.

However, since the subject of your podcast's artwork has come up a few times now, I'd like to quickly address this, and explain what it is and why you'll need it. The art you (or someone else) will design for your show will be featured in places like the iTunes store, and other locations where people will go to access your podcast. Every show should have art associated with it, as it will help you make what you produce look more clean and professional to the public. There are specific sizes, in pixels, that your image will need to be that are considered "industry standards", along with other information that gets a little technical at times, but as you might have guessed, we'll go over all those details in a later chapter.

Finding Your Voice... In Twenty Words or Less

Apart from our discussion about what name you will give your podcast, there is also the question of what the subject will be. For many shows, the name says it all, whereas a show that features your name in the title may not say as much about the content it will feature. The bottom line is that you'll want to have an idea of what your central focus will be, and a way to communicate that consistently to your audience.

If you had been applying the keyword exercise from the last section to your own ideas for a podcast title as you were reading, you may find that you already have a fairly clear idea of what your show will be about. While it may seem that figuring out the focus of your show is really simple, there are a number of things that can actually make this more difficult than you think, and sometimes without the host even being fully aware of it. One example would be if, over time, you begin to incorporate new themes or subjects into your show. I would argue that most podcasts begin to broaden the range of topics they address once they've been at it for a few years, for the simple reason of needing to find fresh content. However, if you begin to deviate *too much* from the subjects central to the interests of your audience, you may find that the response from the podcast's listenership is unfavorable, and you could even lose some of your listeners as a result. A science-themed show might discuss history from time to time, for example, but it wouldn't necessarily be the right show to feature a seven-part series on the Revolutionary War. Then again, if the idea here was actually to feature the *science* behind aspects of Revolutionary War technology, etc, there might be a way to cover this subject, and keep your audience happy as well. It's all a matter of learning how to provide content that is both interesting to you *and* your audience, and in a way that keeps your listeners engaged in what you provide.

So with these considerations in mind, a simple idea I like to offer is for you, the prospective podcaster, to try summing up what your show's focus will be *in 20 words or less*. Keeping your description under 20 words will help you to be concise with your description: so keep it nice and tidy, and let's see what you come up with.

Does the description you came up with give you any clearer idea of what your show's main focus will be?

Say It, Don't Fillet It

While we're discussing the process of finding one's "voice", in the very literal sense, it might help to address your *actual* voice for a moment, since the way you come across sounding to people can often make or break your entire presentation. In essence, a lot of people, when they get behind a microphone for the first time, think that the right thing to do is to use speech that's just unnatural sounding, which may range from silly or phony-sounding voices, to overly-scripted dialogue (you know, the stuff that sounds like it's being read off of a sheet of paper... which is probably because it *actually is* being read off a sheet of paper). A lot of people new to podcasting have never really heard what their voices sound like through a quality microphone and a series of preamps, compressors, equalizers, and other processing equipment. A good pair of headphones will only further optimize this experience, and I've often seen in the past that many people's reactions to hearing their own voices for the first time under optimal settings can be quite comical. If people like the way their voice sounds, they often might subconsciously begin to embellish elements of their speech pattern, which can come across sounding overindulgent, or maybe just amateurish. The same can be said of people who are unhappy with how their voice sounds; these individuals sometimes begin altering their voices, and trying to make their voices "sound like a radio host."

If you think you may be doing any of these things, please *stop*, right now. Generally, trying to make your natural speaking voice sound like what you're hearing on the radio, or in other podcasts, will really only make you sound like a jerk. So don't do it.

The only real "trick" to sounding good on a microphone, in my honest opinion, is learning to be yourself, and mastering the use of your natural voice to the best of your abilities. However, there are a few supplemental strategies that can be applied as well:

> As you're learning, you may notice that if you smile when speaking into a microphone, it will improve your enunciation slightly. Try it out, but here again, be careful; you don't want to sound like Jack Nicholson with a giant, hideous, "Brand X" smile glued to your face every time you talk, like he did (and did *so well*) in Tim Burton's 1988 *Batman* film. If this technique helps, that's great, but don't forget that your goal is to sound natural!

> Conversely, it is important to remember that if you're going to sound good on a podcast, maybe there are times where you shouldn't sound *too* natural or relaxed. In other words, the same tonality you might use speaking to your kids, while sprawled along your couch, upside down, with your dog on top of you, probably won't sound too great on the

microphone. Try to put a little more energy behind your "on air" voice than you normally use when speaking, but don't overdo it, and remember that clear, coherent pronunciation of words will help more than anything.

Finally, the old adage, "practice makes perfect" certainly applies here too; if you want to improve how you sound on the microphone, often what will help you the most is simply doing it more. Just keep at it.

Your Past Makes Today's Podcast

Even after all of this talk about why you want to start podcasting, you may still be thinking, "I really want to do a podcast, but I just don't know what to talk about." If that's the case, the first thing I suggest you consider are what natural talents and traits you might consider yourself an expert in. What kinds of jobs have you worked in the past? What is your number one personal hobby? Are there personal experiences you've had in your life that you have a wealth of knowledge about? What other kinds of things can you call yourself an "expert" in? Virtually anything you've done over the course of your life can provide fodder for compelling conversation, or at very least, conversation that *somebody* will find interesting.

The other thing to keep in mind is that, due to the popularity of shows where the host does little more than interview guests to fill out the time, even if you *aren't* an expert in any field, you can still have guests on your podcast that will more than make up for the knowledge you may lack, so long as the questions you ask are good ones. Again, we'll talk more about inviting guests on your podcast, and the art of interviewing them, as well as what technical materials you'll need to be able to do it, a bit later.

Bells & Whistles: The Art of Ear Candy

Above all else that you do as a podcaster, your job is to provide compelling content, and to make that content as listenable as possible. Granted, this doesn't always mean having a sound-treated room, with enough Styrofoam on the walls to make it look like the inside of an egg crate factory. There are many things you can do to give your podcast an aesthetic appeal, which might include what are, at times, less than optimal sound environments. If used creatively, they might even *enhance* the podcast listening experience. For instance, try imagining an interview with a nature expert that's actually recorded in the forest, with nature sounds and the tweeting of little birds providing a bed for the interview. In essence, there are times when using less, but doing it in a creative way, might help make your podcast sound more unique.

Just like some blogs have hardly any pictures and little formatting apart from a white background, a podcast can be as simple as an audio file that you create, featuring your voice, and the voice of others that might include a co-host or a guest. You really don't need much more, although most podcasts feature some kind of theme music or **introduction**, which consists of a piece of music that may include a voiceover read by an announcer that kicks off every program. This introduction helps set the tone of the show, and eases the listener into a state of mind where their world, for the next hour or so (or however long your podcast is) becomes the world you create.

Having a concluding piece of music, or perhaps the same music as what you use at the show's beginning, is also helpful. This **outro** at the end of the program (as they began to be referred to in television and radio during the 1970s) presents a natural ending to the podcast, and paired with the intro, can help package your show in a nice sounding template that your listeners can come to recognize and expect as a sort of "format" for your podcast.

Using music on various portions of a podcast can also improve the sound and quality, if it is employed tastefully. A quiet bed of music behind certain places where a person is talking can add mood or ambience to that part of the show, or it can also lead up to a **segue** (pronounced *seg-way*, just like those dorky two-wheeled thingies that look like giant pogo sticks on wheels that you see people riding from time to time in cities). This is basically any section added to your show that allows you, and your listeners, to take a short break during your podcast, generally using a minor musical transition.

A quick note about the music you'll use (which we'll address more in depth a bit later) has to do with copyright and royalties. You can't use just *any* song you want on your podcasts, since using popular music without obtaining proper permission is an infringement of copyright law. Because of the laws that protect artists from having their work used without permission or royalties paid, podcasters do need to be aware that certain audio you may want to have in your show must either be used after permission is obtained, or the use of public domain alternatives will have to suffice instead. Fortunately, there are many resources for free music that can be found online, featuring audio files that generally require little more than acknowledgement of their creator, and a link back to their website. Among places you can find royalty free music on the web are sites like www.freemusicarchive.org, as well as www.stockmusic.net. Even more simply, a search on YouTube for royalty free music will often bring back countless results, but be careful that you read the guidelines under each video's description, and make sure the creator has stated that the music is free to use, and whether they request a link back to their page, etc.

I Swear: The Use of Profanity on Podcasts

Whether or not you should include profanity on your podcast is another topic that often seems to be overlooked in discussion, and it's an important one for a number of reasons. In a lot of ways, the podcasting medium exemplifies freedom of speech and expression, as well as the ideals of **new media**, a general term for modern on-demand access to content using digital devices, and the generation of new and unregulated content in near or actual real-time. Due to the absence of regulation by agencies like the Federal Communications Commission (FCC), podcasters are given a unique platform to address whatever topics we choose, and to use whatever language suits us in doing so.

A number of very popular podcasts do use profanity today, but let's face it: these days, the use of harsh language is far more acceptable than in decades past. Or maybe we've just grown more accustomed to hearing it. Whatever the case, using profanity on your podcast probably won't get you blacklisted and booted off the web. However, it could still cause problems for you, if you aren't careful.

According to the *Frequently Asked Questions For Podcast Makers* featured at the iTunes website, "References to illegal drugs, profanity, or violence in the podcast title, description, or cover art" may actually lead to the podcast being rejected by iTunes. Furthermore, the FAQ states that it is forbidden that podcasts use "explicit language in the podcast when the <explicit> tag is not set to 'yes'." Hence, while explicit content is accepted by iTunes, you'll need to choose whether your show will feature such language and content, and be sure to designate it as such.

Another element worthy of addressing about explicit language has to do with terrestrial radio and other FCC regulated mediums; but what, you may ask, does a podcast have to do with any of these? Due to a demand for new content paired with a lack of funds needed to pay talent, there are many instances where smaller terrestrial radio stations will rebroadcast podcasts as part of their daily lineup. I have had a few stations do this with podcasts I produce, which on a few occasions has resulted in emails from program directors reminding me that, if the shows are to continue airing on their stations, they must be 100% FCC compliant (I generally tend to do this anyway, out of habit, after years of annual tests with what's called "responsible broadcast initiative" training in the radio industry. Then again, I guess we all have our moments). While I never incorporate any foul language into those shows that I know will broadcast terrestrially, there are certain subjects that, depending on how they are addressed, may still constitute a problem if not handled carefully.

A final consideration about swearing has to do with how doing so might actually affect the quality of your show, and even how the listener perceives you. I was discussing this subject with Kyle Philson and Cam Hale of the *Expanded Perspectives* podcast a while back. These fellows are a couple of very laid back Texans who discuss ancient history and unexplained phenomena on their show, and I was kind of surprised to learn how adamant they both were about not using foul language on their programs. At one point Kyle offered, "If you go to a bar with me, yeah I'm gonna swear. But when it's live and time to produce the show, we won't swear a bit." Cam added that, "when you listen to how much swearing some podcasts use, to me it makes those hosts sound less intelligent, whether or not I know that to be the case."

It's an interesting point they made: can the language you use actually give your listeners a false impression about your knowledge and overall reliability as a host? The short answer is *yes*, so proceed with caution if you decide to incorporate explicit language into your podcast, and though it may sound contradictory, if you *do* use profanity, try to be tasteful about it (which I believe can be done).

Know Your Audience, Know Yourself

Lastly, as a podcaster it is important to know your audience. There may be times where you'll go through periods where you seem to get little, if any, feedback from your listenership. Often, the old saying "no news is good news!" holds true here: don't be discouraged if you aren't getting huge amounts of feedback from listeners in the form of emails, reviews on iTunes, Facebook Likes, and Twitter interactions, since it seems true that people are far more likely to contact you when they are *dissatisfied* about something, rather than just to reach out and say "job well done." Understanding this early on can be helpful, since many podcasters will launch their shows with great aspirations (and often unrealistic ones) of taking the world by storm.

Depending on how you produce and promote what you do, as well as the kinds of subjects you choose to address, you may indeed grow a huge following in no time, but it is more likely that gaining followers will be a slow and gradual process. The more people you reach, the more people you'll hear from; and rest assured, for as many people that let you know they admire and appreciate what you do, there will at least be a handful that take issue with you, whether or not it's entirely justified, and will seem to work very hard at making life a living hell for you just because they can. Every audio glitch, background noise, or comment you make that they disagree with will be fodder for another attack or criticism. They may even think it is their duty, as a listener, to help you grow and learn by posting nagging comments or negative reviews about your program on social media, iTunes and other places.

Your first reaction to this may be anger, or even despair and hopelessness at the thought of what you're doing as a waste of time, and one that sucks more wind than you ever realized, prompting you to consider tossing in the proverbial towel. But here are a few things to consider when this important moment of self-realization eventually does come around:

➤ Despite the harshness of your critics and their words, ask yourself: do they still convey things about your show that, by listening to what they've said, may help you improve what you're doing? Don't always shrug off your critics and their opinions, because what they're saying may offer you a chance to grow and actually sharpen what you do, and how you do it.

➤ By the same token, don't forget that some people are just complainers. While you may learn from some critiques you receive, try not to take them too terribly to heart, and learn to recognize when a complaint about your show is really just a person being whiny.

➤ If a person decides to engage you directly about something they dislike about your show, you can use this as an opportunity to ask what kinds of things they might prefer to hear that would improve the show in their eyes. You may even generate some unique new ideas by doing so, and in my experience, nine times out of ten, the complainer will soften their attacks once you respond, if you have done so in a tactful, understanding way.

Regarding negative feedback you may receive, an interesting experiment you can try with iTunes reviews of your podcast as they begin to appear over time (and I'll bet this is something that many podcasters may never even realize they had the option of doing) is to look at what people in other countries say about your show. This can be done by opening iTunes and navigating to the iTunes store, then scrolling to the bottom of the window and clicking the round country flag icon in the bottom right hand corner. This will allow you to select the country or region you wish to view, and thus access reviews from other parts of the world once you navigate to your show's page. Interestingly (or not surprisingly), a trend I have found is that people in America seem to leave the majority of the negative feedback on podcasts!

Let's consider this carefully for a moment: does it indicate that Americans are more picky and ungrateful in general? Conversely, are people in the U.S. just more honest about how they feel? Based on the wording of a lot of the negative reviews online, my own personal theory is that, thanks to the shroud of anonymity afforded us by the Internet, some people simply find it empowering to be able to lash out and attack others in various online forums, and with few, if any, repercussions. It doesn't take a rocket scientist to pick up on how this usually indicates more about *the attackers* than it does the objects of those attacks. For whatever reason, this is especially the case in the Western World, and as a result of people's fickle nature and general lust for instant gratification, we have an interesting social phenomenon that seems to manifest in people being jerks a lot of the time. This is especially the case online, and yes, it happens very often here in America. I don't mean to generalize here, but I do recommend you try the experiment I've described, and take a look at how responses tend to differ in various parts of the world. I bet you'll see what I mean.

There may be more that could be said, but as far as important things I think a prospective podcaster should consider *before* getting into the thick of things, the points we've discussed in this chapter are among the most relevant. So enough of the philosophical waxing; now let's take a look at how a podcast is produced, and what tools you'll need to actually make it happen while keeping your budget in mind, as well as your long-term goals as a podcaster.

CHAPTER TWO: CREATING A PODCAST

Congratulations, you've just broken free like a spring butterfly from what some here in the industry affectionately call the "pre-casting" phase: a bizarre, larval stage that precedes any actual podcasting. Before that, you may also have gone through a period of moping around complaining about how you've always *wanted* to be a podcaster, but that you would never manage to decipher all the technical knowledge one needs in order to do it. As we both know by now, that's not *really* the case, but the technical hurdles can still seem daunting at times.

So in this chapter, we'll look at the kinds of hardware and online resources you'll need in order to actually create and edit your podcast, as well as how and where to upload it and make it available to the world.

The creation of a podcast isn't really all that complex. In fact, the process is relatively simple, and involves these basic steps:

- Plan what you will want to discuss on the episode you're about to record, and arrange to connect with any guests or co-hosts before you begin

- Connect your microphone to a computer, launch the device or audio software you'll be using to record the show (and make sure that the software recognizes your microphone or hardware as the primary recording device), and begin recording

- Save the completed audio file once you've finished recording, and make any edits that may be required

- Tag the audio file with a show title, artwork, the names of the hosts, and any similar **metadata** that you may wish to add

- Upload the file to the website of the hosting service you use to store your audio

- Copy the direct link to the file's location on the hosting service site once the upload is complete, and add this link to your show's website so that your RSS feed will update podcast directories like iTunes with your latest show

Some of the details in this brief outline I've given you may sound like complete German (unless you speak German, and therefore you know I'm bluffing, or that maybe I'm just really bad when it comes to German language). We'll explain every step of the process more in depth in just a bit, but now that we've covered the basic steps involving how a podcast is produced, let's take a look at the actual tools you'll need to make it happen:

> First, you'll need a modicum of equipment, which will include a microphone, a computer, and a way to connect the two. Conveniently, some computers actually have a microphone already built into them; however, this kind of microphone isn't ideal for making a podcast. Still, there are certain computers with built-in-microphones that would at least create passable, or maybe even decent-sounding audio. Ideally, you'll want to use a small mixing console and an assortment of audio cables to connect an external microphone into your computer. Alternatively, you could purchase a USB microphone, designed with

its own USB cable interface that will allow it to be plugged directly into your computer.

➢ You'll also need a computer program that will allow you to record the show and edit the audio file afterward (although there are many podcasters that prefer to record onto a standalone recording device, rather than using a computer program, which I'll explain later). There are free and paid-for versions of audio recording software that can be obtained online, and some decent editing programs may even be included with the computer you own (this is usually the case if you are a Mac user, for instance, which comes equipped with the **Garage Band** audio recording program).

➢ Other programs you will likely need when podcasting are those used to communicate with other people, either directly between two computers, or by calling a telephone. **Skype** is the most popular among these programs, and while alternatives exist, the popularity of using Skype to connect hosts with their guests during interviews, or even just to connect two or more hosts who live far apart, has become nearly unrivaled. While certain services associated with Skype may cost a small amount, the program itself, as well as the majority of its features, are absolutely free, and can be downloaded onto any computer.

> Finally, a decent pair of headphones is a must for any podcaster, as you'll never be able to gauge the sound of your voice, how it's coming across on the microphone, and other elements of your overall mix without these.

With the processes and equipment I've outlined here fresh on our minds, now we will look at how it can all be used to create a podcast using entirely free services and programs on the web. By doing so, you'll see that getting into podcasting doesn't have to cost you hundreds, or even *thousands* of dollars. However, I do want to be clear in saying that none of the free options we're about to look at will give you *optimal* capabilities as a podcaster. If you're thinking of getting into things a bit more seriously, and you have an excellent, high-quality production in mind for what you envision yourself doing, it's still good to know about the "cheap" methods we're about to look at, and the usefulness of some of the services that will be outlined. Of greater help to you, however, will be the more advanced concepts we're going to look at later, after we discuss the basics of podcasting in their simplest (and least expensive) essence.

Tools of the Trade: Building a Podcast Arsenal on a Budget

Many successful entrepreneurs know the time-tested rule that making a profit often involves spending money first. The same is true of anything you really want to put quality behind: you're going to have to spend a little money in order to get things off the ground. However, one of coolest things about podcasting, especially for part-timers and hobbyists who do it for fun, or maybe just as an excuse to get together with buddies, pound back a beer, and nerd out over their favorite television shows, movies, sports teams, or what's happening in the world at large, is that it doesn't have to cost much apart from the microphones and computers you'll need; these are the bare essentials of podcasting.

First off, I'm going to make just a few general recommendations about equipment you'll need for podcasting, with specific interest in assembling a list of essentials that will help save you money, but will also get you decent audio quality on a budget. Of course, I want to be clear that in outlining a few of these different pieces of equipment for you below, I do not receive any "kickbacks" or other rewards or benefits for these recommendations; my choice to include them here is based solely on practical considerations pertaining to their use, and with interest in helping someone less experienced with audio equipment make quality purchases.

When we begin fleshing out more "advanced" podcasting approaches later in the book, at that time we'll go over a broader range of high quality equipment that any serious podcaster would swear by. In fact, there will be a section appropriately titled "The War Room" where we look at how to assemble a truly formidable studio right in your own home—perhaps one of even *dangerous* capabilities (there's a reason why, among friends, my personal studio is known as "The Bunker"; it contains enough computers, audio interfaces, microphones, cables, and general junk to rival the console room of the TARDIS... but as time travelers tend to do, I'm getting ahead of myself).

For now, if you are on an extremely limited budget, you'll still need a computer, and a way to connect it to the Internet; fortunately, nowadays most people have access to this. If sound quality isn't a huge concern for you (although it *should be*, plain and simple), and your laptop has a small built-in webcam and microphone, as most do these days, you might be able to get away with using that for your microphone. Personally, I would never recommend this, although in a few rare, last minute circumstances, the built-in microphone on my MacBook Pro has served quite well in creating listenable audio. The trick here is to get fairly close to your microphone, generally about 4 to as much as 12 inches away, but not so close that distortion occurs. Then again, I'd argue that if you happen to be using a computer with a microphone that's even remotely worthy of consideration for use in a podcast, then you can probably afford to spend the $50 a decent microphone would cost, which is the budget I've chosen to set for our present foray into the "least expensive" options.

The simplest solution in terms of being both cost effective, and also less involved from a technical standpoint, is to go with a USB microphone that will plug directly into your computer (keep in mind, however, that while this is cost effective, I generally advise against running a microphone directly into a computer, since using a mixing board as your interface will improve your sound, and allow you to have much more control over the audio you record). A number of models that are inexpensive can be purchased online for as little as $49.99, offered by companies like Samson, Audio-Technica, and Blue.

I've listed a couple of these below, which presently fall between the $50-$60 price range:

➢ **Samson C01U USB Studio Condenser Microphone**: This microphone has a pretty straightforward design, and is compatible with most audio programs and interfaces. Keep in mind, however, that a **condenser** microphone like the C01U can tend to pick up a fair amount of room noise; this hasn't kept them from being used by a number of podcasters, and I have used them in the past without too much trouble.

➢ **Blue Snowball Ice USB Microphone**: This charming little microphone sits right on your desk on a simple little tripod stand, and is capable of recording HD audio.

Another option is to use a less-expensive microphone that is not USB enabled, and connect it to your computer with a separate USB interface. The **Audio-Technica ATR2USB** is one such device, which converts a 3.5mm plug to a USB input that can plug directly into your computer. Using an adapter like this paired with a simple **dynamic** microphone (a close-pattern microphone that, unlike a condenser, picks up sound only right around the mouthpiece) might offer an even more cost-effective option for assembling your budget-constrained podcasting arsenal. If implemented properly, I have known a few podcasters who were able to use a system similar to what I've described here to get surprisingly good audio quality with their shows.

While we're on the subject of USB microphones, there is another device Audio Technica offers that I want to mention. The **Audio-Technica AT2005USB** is a microphone that features both cable *and* USB outputs. This allows you the ability to use the mic either by plugging it directly into a device with a USB cable, or you can use an XLR microphone cable to plug it directly into a mixer. The microphone sells for a little more than $50 through most retailers online, making it both an affordable, and versatile option.

While having USB functionality can be helpful, at times, it generally won't matter if your microphone can connect with USB if you choose to use a mixer in your setup instead. While this introduces a few additional technical elements into how your podcast is produced, these aren't difficult to master, and as I have already touched on, using a small mixing board will also give you a greater degree of control over the sound you produce.

The simplest varieties of mixing consoles usually involve a two-channel interface, one of which you plug your microphone into, and the other you can use for a co-host, or for an audio source you might use for sound effects coming from your computer. Arguably, the most popular of these lower-end mixers among podcasters is the **Behringer Xenyx 502**, which like the Blue Snowball microphone listed above, can be bought for a little less than $50, although I've occasionally seen even cheaper models than this one.

If you think that the microphone-mixer combo is the route you'll want to take, but you're still concerned about your budget, one excellent (and cost-effective) solution offered by the same company, Behringer, is their **PODCASTUDIO-USB Podcasting Bundle**, which contains the mixer above, along with a dynamic microphone and stand, a pair of closed-back headphones, a USB interface, and all the cables necessary to connect the various equipment to your computer; you can literally begin podcasting right out of the box, and this decent little start-up package sells online for around $99.

In addition to being made available with free shipping at a number of online retailers, the bundle I've just described also includes a download code for a free copy of Tracktion 4 DAW audio software that works with either Mac or PC, which will allow you to edit the audio you record. In fact, most recording interfaces you can buy come with either a disc that allows you to install a similar program, or as has become more popular today with everything moving to the "cloud" as it has, a download link to obtain the program.

Granted, you don't need a disc or any special download link to obtain decent quality audio recording software. There are many programs available online that are either free or very reasonably priced for download, and depending on the kind of podcast you'll be doing, you will likely need at least a few of these, which we'll take a look at now.

Popular among podcasters is **Audacity**, an open source audio recording and editing utility that can be downloaded for free at this link:

http://audacityteam.org/download/

Audacity is relatively easy to use, and there are a variety of resources available online for people who have questions or may want to learn additional features that can help improve the sound of their podcast. While Audacity is the first editor I would recommend to podcasters for general use, a few other options include **Ardour**, **Jokosher**, **Traverso DAW**, **RecordForAll**, and **Wavosaur**, but arguably, none quite match the Spartan simplicity Audacity will offer you.

While we're speaking of audio editing software, there are other programs you'll need to get your podcast off the ground and sounding its best. If you aren't an experienced audio engineer, you may find that after recording your show, something like the level of your co-host's microphone had been too low, which caused their audio level to be noticeably quieter than yours. In truth, there are any number of things that can cause levels to be all over the place in a recording you've made, and early on in my podcasting career, I had certain listeners who would constantly complain about how quiet my co-hosts were (or maybe it was just that I naturally speak more loudly than they do). I was able to overcome this problem with the inclusion of a bit of audio processing, in addition to generally leveling the microphones better with a pre-show "sound check"; something I still do before *every* show I record. These elements help me to consistently achieve balanced-sounding recordings. However, there are actually programs (and yes, free ones!) that will balance the audio levels of your recording for you, which can be a tremendous help to someone who is just learning how to podcast.

The first one, which I have recommended for years, is called **Levelator**. However, its creators announced in late 2012 that they had ceased to update it, although versions can still be downloaded online for both Windows and Mac at this link: http://www.conversationsnetwork.org/levelator/ (note that the link above will actually redirect you to www.webarchive.org, likely due to the software's AWOL status with regard to updates ceasing like they did). After installing Levelator, it works by opening the program, and simply dragging an audio file into the Levelator logo that pops up; but something to remember is that it only works with WAV or AIFF file formats, which can tend to create larger files once your show has been processed (we'll talk about how to convert these to smaller mp3 format files later).

Some people prefer not to use Levelator these days, since it's no longer regularly updated. There is an equally useful (no, *far more useful*) service that I would recommend as an alternative, provided by www.auphonic.com. In addition to normalizing the audio levels of your file, with an Auphonic account you are able to deploy your audio files automatically to storage services and sites like YouTube, Amazon S3, Archive.org, Soundcloud, and Libsyn. So in essence, you upload your files to Auphonic, which then "brings your audio and video files up to a professional sound quality, encodes the result to your preferred combination of output files, and distributes these to the service(s) of your choice," as explained at the Auphonic website. While Auphonic does charge for their services beyond a certain point, it is possible to use a majority of their services at little or no cost. You can learn more about how it works with this helpful podcasting tutorial they've put together, that deals with some of the same elements we've discussed about free podcasting: https://auphonic.com/blog/2013/02/07/how-to-podcast-for-free/.

Earlier in this chapter, we already touched on **Skype**, and why it will become among your most important tools as a podcaster (apart from becoming an important part of many people's lives outside its usefulness with things including audio recording, journalism, and the like). Just to recap, here are a few of the ways it may prove to be useful for you:

> ➤ Skype will allow you to call guests, as well as co-hosts, for free

> ➤ You can use Skype to take calls from your listeners if you also decide to stream your podcast as a live show while recording

> ➤ Skype features affordable calling plans that will allow you to make calls to virtually all parts of the world, in the event that you wish

to interview a guest who lives in another country

The primary Skype features that are useful to podcasters require little prior technical knowledge, and are generally part of the free version. All you have to do is download the program onto your computer from www.skype.com.

Another helpful program to have is one that will allow you to record your Skype calls. For PC users, **Pamela for Skype** is a free program that allows you to record both audio, and video onto your computer. It can be obtained easily by downloading it at http://www.pamela.biz/en/. For Mac users, the downside is that you generally will have to pay to have audio software that will record more than 10 minutes of audio at a time (although there are other ways to record audio, rather than using Skype call recording software, as I'll address in a moment). **Call Recorder** for Skype is one of the most popular options, and you can try it free for seven days, after which a license is $29.99. You can purchase it at http://www.ecamm.com/mac/callrecorder/.

Rogue Amoeba offers two alternatives, **Piezo** and **Audio Hijack**, for which free versions are made available that limit up to 10 minutes of consecutive audio recording, before a layer of static is added to the recording, making it essentially unusable (and hence the necessity for purchasing the full version to unlock longer recording abilities). Audio Hijack is by far the more versatile of the two, and the cost upgrade to the full version will run you about $32. For those who have budget in mind, Piezo is a little simpler to use, and a license for the full version that allows non-stop audio recording costs only $15—by far one of the best deals for Mac users. You can pick up any of Rogue Amoeba's software at their website, www.rogueamoeba.com/.

There is one program I have found that offers free recording of Skype calls on both Windows *and* on Mac, and that's called **Callnote Regular**, which can be downloaded from it's parent company's site at http://www.kandasoft.com/. I mention this one last because I have not personally tested or used this program enough in the past to recommend whether it functions on par with the others I've detailed above; but it features a number of options, including recording up to eight participants in a call simultaneously, and sending the audio files to a DropBox folder or similar interface as soon as the recording has finished. Alternatively, there is a non-Skype service called www.freeconferencecall.com that may also be useful, which offers free online calling services, and the ability to record those calls.

Programs like these are really only necessary if you need to record audio on the same computer that your Skype call originates from (although keep in mind, some of them, like Audio Hijack Pro, can be used to capture audio from sources other than Skype, like a media player in a browser window, etc. This can be very handy, but do keep copyright considerations in mind when it comes to the kinds of audio you capture, such as the use of popular music, which nearly always requires proper licensing for replay).

If you have more than one computer handy, and you are using a mixer in your podcasting setup, you can use one computer to initiate Skype calls with guests and co-hosts, from which audio is sent back through your mixer. Then you can install Audacity on your second computer, and send audio from your mixer to that computer, thus recording your voice *and* your Skype calls, as well as any other audio you feed through your mixer.

The specifics of this setup will be addressed more in depth later, but for now, the way this works is to send an audio cable from the headphone output on your computer running Skype, and plug that into a channel on your mixing board. Then you'll want to send one of the audio outputs from your mixer *back to the Skype computer's microphone input*, which will allow the person on Skype to hear any audio coming from your mixing board (you may need to go into the "Preferences" tab in Skype and adjust the audio settings so that Skype will recognize the computer's audio input as the source of incoming sounds). It often helps to use one of your mixer's **Aux Sends** as the source for audio sent back to the Skype computer, which I'll explain later in the section about how a mix/minus configuration works. By doing this, your Skype caller will be able to hear your voice as it is picked up by the microphone plugged into your board, and you'll hear them (and your own voice) through the headphones plugged into the "Phones" jack on your mixer. Finally, you will run audio from another of the audio outputs on the mixer (there are usually several of these, but here I would recommend the **Tape Out**) and send that to the microphone/audio input on the computer with Audacity. This will allow you to record both your voice, and the Skype call, into the Audacity session you have opened. If you do happen to have more than one computer handy, this is one of the most flexible ways to record your shows, with no additional costs required for buying recording software.

One more option that works well so far as recording your Skype calls is to use a separate audio recording device, such as a portable digital recorder, to record the audio sent from your board in the same manner described above. Cliff Ravenscraft, a guy otherwise known to podcasters everywhere as the "Podcast Answer Man," highly recommends using this method of recording, since having a small audio device with its own power source eliminates the possibility that your computer may die, or that a power outage might occur, potentially destroying hours of podcasting you may have been working on. Cliff is absolutely one of the most knowledgeable podcasting experts there is... *period*. So if he suggests something, I strongly recommend you give it some serious thought (he also sells podcasting equipment at his website, www.podcastanswerman.com, which will help you find the kinds of equipment he recommends at very reasonable prices). Good quality digital recorders, which are essentially those capable of recording in high quality audio formats, and connecting to a computer with USB to download those files later, are generally much less expensive than buying a secondary computer.

However, in the truest spirit of "maverick podcasting," I'll also point out that gaining access to secondary or spare computers for an inexpensive recording rig like this is often easier than you might think. Used or refurbished computers can be bought online for reasonable prices, or even found in places like consignment stores, Goodwill locations, or through classified ads in your town. Or even better yet, you may have friends or family members that would be happy to unload an old "useless" desktop or laptop once they've upgraded. All that's usually required beyond that would be a quick virus scan with free antivirus software like **Avast**, a disc defragmentation on the computer's hard disk to consolidate space and improve performance, and maybe also the removal of old programs you won't need that are merely taking up additional space (or, if messing with computers isn't your thing, most computer repair shops are glad to help you get an older computer running more smoothly). Voilà, you now have a spare computer on hand, which in case anything ever happens to your primary, you can use as a backup if needed. I've found that having older, otherwise "outdated" computers handy that I generally use only for things like audio playback, recording, running a separate Skype account, or other simple tasks, can be very helpful in a pinch.

One more thing to keep in mind about using Skype, despite whatever recording technique you employ, is that with video chat enabled, you may run the risk of degrading your audio quality slightly due to bandwidth considerations. If you don't have an exceptionally fast Internet connection, my first recommendation would be to contact your service provider, and upgrade today so that you won't have as many issues while working with audio over an Internet connection. If that isn't an option for you right now, turning off video and using Skype for "audio only" will help optimize the resources being allotted by your computer, and ensure a clear, reliable audio signal for the duration of the interview you will record.

And while we're discussing video chats with Skype, it stands to reason that you may prefer using video when you're talking with a friend, or speaking with a significant other you haven't seen in a few days. Guests you'll be inviting on your program, on the other hand, may not appreciate having to get all dolled up just so they will look their best on camera during the interview. Unless you've alerted your potential guest beforehand that the interview will require video (and we'll discuss video podcasts a bit later in this book), my advice is to respect your guest's privacy, and stick with "audio only" calls. Skype has separate buttons for each of these calling modes.

Another free program that may come in handy for you is **iTunes**. This one is so obvious that I've found many podcasters overlook it, simply because they think of iTunes only as a program for downloading and playing music and podcasts they want to listen to. However, with iTunes, you can also create playlists, add audio to them, and then arrange them in the order you would like them to be played, as well as automate them to play sequentially by checking the boxes beside each audio file in the lists you compose. This is basically the same way automated **spot blocks** are fired using digital radio automation programs like RCS NexGen, which is currently used by over 2500 radio stations in the United States. With iTunes, not only can you arrange and automate playlists of audio, but you can double click on any individual file to play it as well. With the same Skype recording setup using two computers that I've described above, you could use iTunes as a simple, free audio source from which you can fire sound bytes, royalty free music, and other audio during your program.

I've found a surprising number of podcasters and online radio enthusiasts who use simple setups like these to produce their shows. As you can see, the essentials of producing a quality podcast can be obtained for under $100, if you already have a computer and Internet access.

Free Online Resources: Flexibility, in a Slightly Restrictive Way

One of the best things about the equipment side of things is that you can always upgrade your devices and software at a later time. Generally, with time you will probably have certain equipment begin to wear out anyway, and therefore certain pieces of hardware will require replacement. Of course, before certain items need to be replaced, you may also decide that you just want to improve the quality of your podcast and the way it sounds, which will entail buying more expensive equipment that can more or less be integrated seamlessly into your podcasting setup, and your listeners will never know the difference (unless what you've changed about your setup improves the sound quality of what you're doing, which is a desirable thing).

What can be a little more difficult to change on down the road, however, are the online resources you'll be using, which essentially involve three elements:

➢ The **website** you'll use to post links to your content online

➢ The **RSS feed** that is submitted to various podcast directories like iTunes

➢ The **file hosting** service you use to actually upload and store your content.

Links to the audio files you create and upload with your file hosting service will be posted on your website, and the RSS feed will then communicate to podcast directories that you have new content available. In most cases discussed in this book, we'll use the blogging program **Wordpress** as the basis for your website, which will actually generate the RSS feed for you (easy, right?). However, using a free Google service like **Feedburner**, you are able to take the native RSS feed your site generates, and point it to a new RSS feed that you will use as the actual feed you'll submit to podcast directories (and while using one RSS feed to create another completely different one may seem like an unnecessary extra step, I'll tell you why it can be beneficial in just a moment).

There are various reasons why it can become problematic to change some of these things later on, and hence why I recommend having at least some idea early on about what you'll want to aim to do with your podcast, and how you'll do it. As we discussed in the first chapter, if you're serious about producing a podcast, either to promote a business you already have, or to generate revenue in other ways, it is important to make provisions for web hosting for your podcast that will incorporate a website you already have, or one you will build. A free blog can be obtained at Wordpress.com that will generate an RSS feed for you, which will work fine for delivering your content to various podcast directories. However, it is important for you to consider whether doing this will require you to have to change the web address people use to find your show later on, should you decide to purchase an actual site for your show, for instance. Here are a few more reasons why.

A free Wordpress.com site, while functional and easy to obtain, will have a URL that looks like this:

your-site-name-here.wordpress.com

This isn't really as professional looking, or as easy to find for that matter, as "**www.your-site-name.com**", is it?

An even more pressing concern if you build a simple site with a free Wordpress account is that your site's RSS feed will change if you decide to upgrade to a new webpage later on, and this can spell bad news indeed. The reason: iTunes and several other podcast directories don't allow you to create an account where you can simply log in and change the RSS feed that supplies them with the current episodes of your podcast. Instead, they usually have a general page where you can submit your show's RSS feed, and if accepted, your show will then appear on their site. Thus, if your show's RSS feed changes, guess what happens to your show's listing on those directories? That's right, your shows aren't being updated any longer. Worst-case scenario, you might have to re-submit your show all over again, which means your followers, who find your show by subscribing to its listing on those directories, will have to be notified that they must re-subscribe, or otherwise update the RSS feed they use to get the show.

Granted, there are technical ways that involve coding on your site's backend, which can forward subscribers to the new RSS feed for you behind the scenes, in the event that you simply can't get around having to change it. This can be a royal pain in the arse though, and frankly, you don't ever want to have to do it (and this is coming from somebody who actually *has* had to do it).

Part of the beauty of using Feedburner, as we'll see shortly, is that it allows you to take the feed your website generates, and submit it through your Feedburner account, which then uses it to generate a *new feed* for your blog or podcast (that's right, you actually choose whether your new feed will be a podcast when you're setting up your Feedburner account). This new feed is what you submit to iTunes, and hence, if at some point you ever decide to move your podcast to a new website, or you need to change the feed that generates your Feedburner podcast feed, it can be easily done. Keep that in mind as we're discussing RSS feeds throughout this book, because having a working RSS feed is of great importance to making sure your podcasts are easily accessible, and that they'll remain that way.

To Feed, or Not to Feed: The Debate Over Whether to Use Feedburner

Despite it's effectiveness, not everyone is a fan of using Feedburner, and in truth, there are a few things that I've learned that add some merit to the anti-Feedburner argument. Back in September of 2012, Feedburner users began to notice some problems with the service, which included errors like the number of subscribers to Feedburner podcast feeds indicating zero values. Further lending to people's concerns, Feedburner had previously deactivated its Twitter account in July of 2012, coinciding with their decision to take down their AdSense For Feeds blog. With consideration for how other Google services like iGoogle had similarly gone the way of the dinosaurs, folks began to get quite concerned about whether Feedburner would be next. Thus, many concerned podcasters began switching their RSS feeds over to services like **Feedblitz,** while Todd Cochrane, CEO of **Blubrry** (a company whose products and services we'll discuss in depth later on), warned people that, "If you were ignorant enough to use FeedBurner in the first place, don't be foolish and switch to a service that is crying wolf and suggesting Feedburner is going away!"

All hell was finally breaking loose, it seemed.

Enter Cliff Ravenscraft, who as you'll remember, is arguably one of the most knowledgeable experts on podcasting, and also an individual who has long championed the use of Feedburner's services. On Friday, September 21st, 2012, Ravenscraft took to his blog and addressed the multitude of concerns surrounding the use of Feedburner, and whether it was going to be the next to be removed from Google's services.

"I still do not believe that Feedburner is going to shut down," Ravenscraft wrote, acknowledging the tech issues they appeared to be experiencing at the time. He went on to say:

> "If at any point, Feedburner stops updating our feeds, which would halt the delivery of our content to our audience, for more than 24 hours, it is at that point that I would begin to have anxiety over this issue."

As of July 2015, at which time this portion of the book you are now reading was being written, Feedburner's services still remain active, and they are also still free, unlike various similar services that, in likelihood, had been banking on Feedburner calling it quits three years ago. So why has Feedburner survived, despite the coming and going of many other Google services? Furthermore, should those who are still using it be worried?

To me, it seems quite evident why Feedburner remains online. At one time, this service was almost requisite for podcasting, since it allowed simple access to features that optimized the way a podcast's RSS feed was delivered to users, which many other platforms just didn't offer at that time. Today, a number of different programs, including **Blubrry's PowerPress plugin**, offer similar services that in many ways even *improve* on what Feedburner had once done better than the rest. However, since Feedburner had once been the industry leader, a number of podcasts that launched prior to the summer of 2012 did what only seemed logical at the time, and went with Feedburner, as was recommended by the majority of experienced podcasters. In turn, there are scads of podcasters today who are still using it.

So imagine what would happen if, all of a sudden, Feedburner ended its services, and no longer offered support to podcasters? Surely they must know how many podcasts rely on its services, and how much backlash would therefore result from taking Feedburner down, without at least offering alternatives to the hordes of us out here who have relied on their service for years. I feel that this is probably why, in likelihood, Feedburner remains active... an entire three years after what many perceived as the likely end of a podcasting era.

Sure, stranger things have happened, and for all you or I may know, we could wake up tomorrow only to find that Feedburner died peacefully in its sleep, and that a sickening number of podcasters all around the globe are now left treading water in an ocean of ungodly technical non-functionality. Add to that the swimming sharks: a host of companies will approach us saying, "see, we told you so... and now, lest ye have plans to catch the lunch specials at Davy Jones's Locker, it's high time you swim toward the light. In other words, do like *The Evil Dead*, and *JOIN US!*"

So to summarize, of course there are going to be risks involved with relying on a particular service to ensure that your podcast is accessible at all times. At present, however, I would also argue that logic seems to dictate—along with several years passing and still no discontinuation of service—that the folks behind Feedburner probably realize that removing the service would be problematic; but that's not to say that it couldn't happen.

Therefore, when it comes to podcasting on a budget, using Feedburner is still, in my opinion, both a reliable, and cost-effective service. There are other services, like Blubrry's PowerPress plugin, that will help you achieve similar results, but you'll also need the complete version of Wordpress installed on server space purchased through a web hosting company in order to gain access to all these features, despite the plugin actually costing nothing to download and install. Personally, while I still use Feedburner for one of my podcasts, there are others for which I have used the feed generated by PowerPress instead, with equal success.

Later in this book, when we get into discussing options for podcasters willing to pay for services to improve quality and functionality, you may indeed want to consider alternatives to using Feedburner that include PowerPress, or other options like the aforementioned Feedblitz.

For reasons similar to those already discussed here, I would also like to warn you about the downside to using certain other podcasting services online, as far as things relate to your RSS feed. It may seem like it would be a lot simpler and more effective to go with one of the numerous blog-hosting programs online that feature automated services, which allow you to do things like call in with so little as a telephone and produce your podcast that way. Of course, these services are designed so people who haven't got microphones, or who aren't very tech-savvy, can still produce podcasts. However, as many experts will warn you—including our pal Cliff Ravenscraft—using services like these can lead to your site's RSS feed being "held hostage." In other words, if you start out with one of these services, and decide you later want to switch to self-hosting and keep your RSS feed, they may actually prevent you from being able to do it.

The long and the short of it here is that if you really are dead-set on podcasting inexpensively, sticking with the procedure I'm about to outline will offer you the most clear and simple solutions. It will also allow for changes later if you decide to upgrade to paid services, like we'll discuss when we get to the portion of the book about buying a hosting plan, and building your own website for your podcast. It's not as hard as it sounds, and you'll be glad you did it once your show has found an audience of thousands who expect quality content from you on a consistent basis.

Taking the Freeway: Podcasting Made Easy, and Inexpensive

As we discussed earlier, the three primary elements that will come into play with your podcast are the website (or blog, essentially) and the RSS feed it produces, along with the actual location where you'll store your audio files online. For purposes of this guide, we will be focusing on a free blog with Wordpress.com, and of course, an RSS feed redirected through Google's Feedburner. The audio files you'll be producing will be uploaded and stored at Archive.org.

To create your Wordpress account, first you'll want to visit https://signup.wordpress.com/signup/ and submit the following information:

> Your email address

> The username you'll want for your account

> A password to access it, and

> The blog address for your podcast's site

The **blog address** is the actual domain name you'll choose, with "**.wordpress.com**" appearing on the end of it. Do note, however, that during signup a blue dropdown to the right of this field will offer you a number of options to purchase a .com, .org, .biz, or other more personalized account starting at as little as $18 annually. This may be a reasonable option for some people, and while the fee is inexpensive, I still recommend not going this route if you're looking to buy a domain, and hold out instead for a hosting plan that will allow you a fuller sense of control over what you're doing online. Granted, Wordpress.com will allow you to try out any of their upgrades of this sort for free for a period of 14 days, if you ever want to get a feel for things before you commit to buy.

While there are alternatives to Wordpress like **Blogger**, I would argue that the popularity of using Wordpress for podcast RSS feed generation has led to it becoming optimized somewhat as a platform for podcasters (point in case, I can't think of any friends of mine in the podcasting community who *don't* use it as the backend of their podcast sites... but that isn't to say that *nobody* anywhere is using the alternatives that exist).

Since this book isn't a "how to guide" for Wordpress, I won't go into all the details about how this program works right here. I will, however, recommend to you the **Wordpress Codex**, a sort of online manual that is constantly growing and being updated by other users. You can find it online at this link: http://codex.wordpress.org/Main_Page. There, you'll be able to find out anything you could ever hope to imagine about Wordpress, and how to best implement its features with your podcast in mind.

One thing to keep in mind about having a free Wordpress account like this is that it won't allow you the use of the multitude of **plugins** that become available to those who download the program from

Wordpress.org and install it on their own servers. These plugins are add-ons that perform various functions, and can be downloaded freely (though in some cases, developers will charge a one-time fee for their plugin, like a few of the more advanced examples I'll discuss later in relation to monetizing your podcast).

There are a variety of great plugins made especially for use with podcasting, like the **Blubrry PowerPress Podcasting plugin**, which provides an entire interface within Wordpress for your podcast, and helps it communicate information properly with Feedburner or iTunes. Namely, what this plugin does that has so many podcasters jumping for joy is it creates a simple way to get an RSS feed that solely features the podcasts you link to your site, rather than all the content you post there. That way, if you want to post other things on your site's main feed (like blog posts, etc), that information isn't shared with iTunes and other directories; only your podcasts are.

Since I'm saving our broader discussion of plugins until we get into advanced podcasting in the chapters that follow, the simplest way to get your podcast episodes to be included on your site's primary feed is to create a new post in your Wordpress Dashboard, and include a link to that file in the body of the post. I'll flesh this process out for you more in a moment, but first let's talk about how to find your new Wordpress site's RSS feed.

Feed Me, Seymour! Setting Up Your Feed the Right Way

Once you've completed the signup process with your Wordpress account, you should be able to visit the URL for your site, and after the last forward slash, you'll want to add "**feed/**", which will make your URL look like this:

"your-site.wordpress.com/feed/"

If you visit that link, you'll be taken to a new page that features the raw XML file for your RSS feed, which usually looks something like this:

This XML file does not appear to have any style information associated with it. The document tree is shown below.

```
<rss xmlns:content="http://purl.or
g/rss/1.0/modules/content/" xmlns:
wfw="http://wellformedweb.org/Comm
entAPI/" xmlns:dc="http://purl.org
/dc/elements/1.1/"xmlns:atom="http
://www.w3.org/2005/Atom" xmlns:sy=
"http://purl.org/rss/1.0/modules/s
yndication/" xmlns:slash="http://p
```

```
url.org/rss/1.0/modules/slash/"xml
ns:georss="http://www.georss.org/g
eorss" xmlns:geo="http://www.w3.or
g/2003/01/geo/wgs84_pos#" xmlns:me
dia="http://search.yahoo.com/mrss/
" version="2.0">
```

The URL for the page you are now viewing is the RSS feed address that you'll want to submit to Feedburner when you sign up for your account there. Copy the URL for now, because in a moment you'll be pasting it into a field at the Feedburner page that will "burn a feed" for you.

While Wordpress will generate a feed in the RSS 2.0 format that iTunes recommends, there are other elements your podcast feed must have as well, namely the ability to support what are called **enclosures**. These can be likened to attachments you might include with an email or text message, and much like an image or audio file inserted into the body of an email can be accessed while you're reading the message, having enclosures enabled will allow people who subscribe to your feed to launch the audio directly from their feed reading program or device.

Feedburner will enable these enclosures for your RSS feed with ease, as a part of the process of pointing the URL to your blog's feed, which I'll explain below. However, remember that since Feedburner is a Google service, you may need to log into your Google Gmail account to access it (and if you don't have an account, you can sign up for one easily, whether or not you intend to use the mail account associated with it).

Once you've logged in, go to the following link and proceed from there:

> Visit http://feedburner.google.com

> In the box below where it says, "Burn a feed right this instant", enter your blog's feed URL that you copied earlier. Before you click "Next," *be sure to check the box that says, "I am a podcaster!"* This is important, because doing so is what will enable the enclosures we were just talking about.

> On the screen that follows, there will be boxes where you can enter your **Feed Title** and **Feed Address**. If you wish for the feed title to be something other than the one generated automatically, enter the title you want in this box.

> Next, in the second box below the Feed Title area, you also have the option of changing the end of the Feedburner URL you're creating. They generate one for you, as with

the title, so unless you want something different, this doesn't need to be changed. Once you have the information you want in each of the boxes, click "Next" to activate your new Feedburner feed.

➤ Copy your new feed (which will look like this: **http://feeds.feedburner.com/YourFeed**). This will be the feed you submit to directories like iTunes.

As I described earlier, what we've just done is we've taken your site's feed, and routed it through Feedburner to create (and save) a specific feed for your podcast. Again, if you ever have to change the feed generated by your website, such as if you were ever to change the show's name, or migrate to a new site altogether, you can change this feed in your Feedburner dashboard, *without having to change the feed you submit to iTunes*. Being able to do this, and do it right, may be one of the most important things you'll ever do when it comes to setting up your podcast.

Before we get to how you go about submitting your Feedburner feed to directories, we do need to take into consideration that some people may find your podcast by visiting your Wordpress site. So how do we let these people know that they'll want to subscribe to your show using the Feedburner feed, rather than the site's normal feed?

One of the simplest ways to do this is to use the **Widgets** function to place a link to the new RSS feed in the sidebar of your webpage. From your Wordpress Dashboard, in the left hand column navigate down to "Appearance" and then you'll see "Widgets" in the dropdown. Next you'll be shown a group of widgets that can be dragged from left-to-right and into the sidebar area on your blog, which is the space usually to the left or right of the main content on your Wordpress site. Scroll down until you find the widget labeled "RSS" and drag it over into the position on the sidebar you want it to have. Clicking the arrow on the right hand side of the widget will display options where you can enter the new Feedburner RSS feed, give it a title, and even set the number of items it will display.

Now, before you can do anything else, you've got to find a place where you can store the audio files you'll be creating, so they can be linked to your site.

Upload Complete: Storing Your Audio Files Online

Eventually, once you've recorded the first episode of your podcast and completed any editing that might be required, you'll then need to upload your file to a location on the web where it can be stored, from which a link can be obtained that you'll place in a post on your site. Doing this will send the link to your RSS feed, which will then broadcast the new episode to your subscribers. The question you may be wondering now is, "where do I upload my files so they can be downloaded by my listeners?"

As with all the inexpensive solutions I'm going over for you in this part of the book, there are a few available so far as storage goes just as well. But as you probably guessed, they have their limitations. The first solution that comes to mind is Archive.org, where you can sign up for an account that will allow you to upload files for free. To sign up, visit this link: https://archive.org/account/login.createaccount.php From there, you'll upload your files, copy the direct link back to your file, and post this at your blog (generally, the best way to do this is to **embed** the link within an area of text. For more on how to do this, visit this link to the Wordpress Codex page on embeds: http://codex.wordpress.org/Embeds). Also consider looking at this Wordpress support article on the five primary ways to use Wordpress to share audio: http://en.support.wordpress.com/audio/).

Hosting your audio files with Archive.org will inevitably result in slow download times (this may not be the case if your podcasts are limited to one or two minutes in length, but that's usually not realistic even for those of us with the very least to say; podcasting is, after all, an audible medium built around communication through human speech).

There are a few other free services that may work well for some podcasters, which I will address here. Particularly, these are presented with those in mind who may upload shorter episodes (hence smaller files), or who only do a monthly podcast, which reduces some of the necessities for bandwidth and storage space a bit as well. First among them is **Ourmedia.org**, which I find interesting for a few reasons. They offer unmetered bandwidth, and as a free service. However, they comb through the audio uploaded to their site and remove content that is found to contain what is determined to be third party or inappropriate material, so this is something to consider. Another free service is **Podomatic (**www.podomatic.com) which offers free and paid accounts, as does **Podbean** (www.podbean.com) and **Buzzsprout** (www.buzzsprout.com).

Still in the range of free and inexpensive options, Amazon's **S3** service is a viable consideration, which allows free basic storage, with reasonable fees beyond that. S3 also features add-ons that work with many web browsers that allow easy access for file upload and management; if you are a Firefox user, the **S3Fox Organizer** will allow quick access to your files and storage area from a browser tab. It can be downloaded at http://www.s3fox.net/. Chrome users might also try the **Extended S3 Browser**, which is found at Chrome's web store: https://chrome.google.com/webstore/.

In honesty, I've tried using Amazon's S3 utilities in the past, and while others disagree, I tend to find them a bit clunky, and have never quite managed to get the features to work for me in what seemed like an ideal way. Again, I've known a few podcasters that swear by it, but there are also a few who, like me, have become a bit more wary. Podcaster David Jackson (DavidJackson.org) notes that that in July of 2012, one of his shows, The School of Podcasting, received 25,000 downloads *from his back catalogue alone* (way to go, David!). "Ignoring the amount I would get charged for [my new episodes] in July," he says, "just the bandwidth alone would be $57.63... while Amazon S3 may cheap when you start, it eventually costs you more than Libsyn.com or Blubrry."

Hence, while Amazon S3 is a service that might be a cost-effective storage solution for starters, it can end up becoming very costly as your show begins to gain popularity. I should note, however, that they do provide a monthly calculator at the following link to help you anticipate your costs: http://calculator.s3.amazonaws.com/index.html.

The folks over at Auphonic.com offer a good middle-of-the-road solution to this problem for those intent on podcasting on the cheap, which combines Archive.org's services with Amazon S3: "A good compromise could be to host recent episodes (which usually require more bandwidth) on Amazon S3," they say, "and archive older episodes on Archive.org." Arguably, your newest episodes are going to be the ones that most subscribers will download as they are posted online, within just a few days of the file being posted. If you aren't as worried about random downloads of your back catalog, what Auphonic.com suggests might indeed be a clever way to get around some of the costs you might be facing.

As of the time I began writing this book, a new podcast hosting option has recently launched, at the aptly titled URL www.podcasts.com. This site advertises that they feature free hosting, with unlimited bandwidth, and numerous other features. Admittedly, I haven't had the opportunity yet to scope them out and see whether these features would be ideal for both hobbyists and professional podcasters, so here at the outset, I would say their services are probably at least worth giving a look. They may indeed prove to be an ideal resource for podcasters (and especially those seeking to save a few dollars here and there).

Finally, another way to get your podcasts online for free (although this method will bypass all this emphasis I've been putting on RSS feeds) is to upload them to YouTube. Doing this will require a video editing software program, which will allow you to take an audio file and pair it with images or video so that the file can be uploaded and played from your YouTube profile. Auphonic.com's services will actually upload your files to YouTube for you, and generally I recommend using both the RSS feed method we've been describing, as well as sites like YouTube, where users are likely to find your show at random while searching for other videos. YouTube videos are easy to copy and embed on websites as well, which makes using them another helpful way to consider getting your content out there. In fact, I would argue that so far as free services go, YouTube might rank among the highest in offering a wide array of services for those seeking to produce content and get the word out about it, while still working on a budget.

Just a reminder: as you might have guessed, later we'll go over other audio storage options you should consider, as well as the right and wrong ways to do it, why bandwidth is a consideration, and why I recommend storing your audio with LibSyn.com, a service I've had multiple accounts with, and happily so, for several years now.

Getting Your Podcast on iTunes and Other Podcast Directories

Eventually, once you've recorded the first episode of your podcast and completed all the steps we've outlined thus far, you will want to create a post at your Wordpress site, and link the audio there using the aforementioned techniques found at the Wordpress Codex. This will complete the process of making your first podcast available to the public... congratulations!

However, as we've talked about throughout this chapter, if you really want to make your podcast stand out, you'll need to obtain the kind of reach that can only be provided by having it featured in a directory like iTunes. According to Apple.com's general FAQ on submitting a podcast, getting your show listed in the iTunes Store requires a few specific steps:

> ➢ First, there will need to be at least one episode recorded in either an audio or video format (text documents, in formats like PDF or EPUB, actually qualify too, according to Apple; but these wouldn't really make your

file a podcast, would they?). Your media file can be in any of the following audio or video formats: M4A, MP3, MOV, MP4, or M4V.

➤ As we've already done, iTunes wants you to create an RSS feed that conforms to RSS 2.0 specifications, includes the RSS tags recommended by iTunes, and which points to your episode using the <enclosure> tag (again, don't worry about this if you're working with a Feedburner feed, which as we outlined earlier, optimizes your feed to these specifications).

➤ One thing that you may not have done yet is create cover art for your Podcast, which according to iTunes, must be in either JPEG or PNG file format. They also require that the artwork be in the RGB color space, and according to the latest size and pixilation requirements, a minimum size of 1400 x 1400 pixels and a maximum size of 2048 x 2048 pixels is necessary. Your art must meet these criteria to be approved by iTunes, as well as to qualify for being featured in the iTunes store.

➢ Finally, the RSS feed, cover art, and any episodes you have are posted to a server that, in accordance with iTunes, "supports byte-range requests and a publicly accessible URL. Support for byte-range requests allows users to stream your episodes." Generally, your Wordpress site and Feedburner account will support these elements for you; your artwork can be uploaded to the web (such as the media library in your Wordpress account), and a link to this can then be included in the proper field on your Feedburner account page, so that it will appear along with the RSS feed it produces.

➢ Finally, you will submit your podcast's RSS feed to iTunes.

This may all sound very complex, but you've actually completed most of it already. I'm including this breakdown of the basic requirements iTunes outlines at their website just for good measure. The only elements that we have *not* covered previously that are of concern to you now are as follows:

➢ Creating artwork that meets the 1400 by 1400 pixel requirements iTunes requests

➢ Uploading your artwork (a process we'll describe in depth later in this section)

➢ Submitting your podcast's RSS feed to iTunes

By now, this entire "submitting your podcast to iTunes" thing has probably begun to take on a mythical air about it. I wouldn't be surprised if many of you doubt its existence; much like you would the mythical Sasquatch, that famous and gigantic guardian of the Pacific Northwest's steepest slopes.

Fortunately, getting your podcast listed on iTunes won't be as difficult as capturing decent photos of Bigfoot has proven to be. However, doing so *will* require you to have **the latest version of iTunes**. You can get it here:

https://www.apple.com/itunes/download/

Once you have this, open iTunes, and follow these instructions:

➢ Navigate to the "iTunes Store" button, in the upper-right corner of the window. Click "Podcasts" in the navigation bar

➢ Beneath the words "Podcast" on the right hand side of the page, in the "Podcast Quick Links" section, click "Submit a Podcast".

➢ From here, the instructions on the "Submit a Podcast" page on iTunes will guide you through the rest of the process.

It will usually take a day or so for your podcast to be reviewed so don't despair if you don't hear from them right away.

While we're talking about submitting your podcast feed to iTunes, keep in mind there are a few more directories to which you should consider submitting your podcast as well. I've even had listeners in the past request that they be able to download shows using these alternatives, since not everyone prefers to use iTunes to find and listen to podcasts. Among these directories are **Stitcher** and **TuneIn**, and at the end of this chapter, we will go over each of these, as well as a few other options.

Another part of the submission process is having artwork to go with your podcast's listing on the sites where it will be downloaded. There are some pretty specific criteria that must be met for doing this in most cases, so we'll go over this process now.

Fine Art: Creating iTunes Artwork for Your Podcast

Creating quality artwork for your podcast's listing in places like the iTunes store is one of the most useful ways you can draw attention to your show, as well as advertise to potential subscribers what your show is about, and why they'll want to listen.

In fact, this is precisely what iTunes says with regard to why podcasters need cover art for their shows. "High quality cover art attracts new subscribers to your podcast," their FAQ states, along with the suggestion that a title and brand or source name be incorporated into this artwork. If you browse the iTunes store, you may see that some shows don't feature artwork at all, and I have known podcasters in the past that fell into this category; in one instance, the host had often claimed to have thousands and thousands of listeners; I've looked at the show's reviews, and the fact that they have no iTunes cover art, and find serious credibility issues with these claims.

Just ask yourself, "how professional does a book appear without a cover?" The cover is an integral part of the packaging that helps sell a book, and podcasts are no different. While in some cases it may not be *absolutely* required to submit cover art, it is nonetheless highly recommended... so much that, in my opinion, you might as well go ahead and consider it mandatory.

There are some specifications for cover art that you'll want to keep in mind, which we touched on earlier in the section about how to submit your feed to iTunes. For reference, here they are again in their simplest essence:

> Create your cover art in either JPEG or PNG file format

> The artwork must also be in RGB format

> Currently, size and pixilation requirements state that a minimum size of 1400 x 1400 pixels and a maximum size of 2048 x 2048 pixels must be used, so that the image (which will appear much smaller when displayed online) will meet image quality standards for older monitors, as well as newer screens like Apple's Retina displays

Again, it's important for your art to meet these criteria to be approved by iTunes, and while some shows, as I mentioned before, may choose not to feature any cover art, it's important to remember that in order to qualify for being an occasional "featured podcast" in the iTunes store (such as when a podcast begins to gain a large following, at which time they may be included in a special listing called "What's Hot"), you'll have to follow these guidelines.

We also mentioned earlier that the artwork you create, along with the RSS feed, must then be made available using a server that supports byte-range requests, and which features a publicly accessible URL. As you might have guessed, your Wordpress site and Feedburner account will support these elements for you, so here's a quick summary of how you'll do that:

> Navigate to the "Media" tab on your Wordpress Dashboard, then click "Add New" in the dropdown, and drag the artwork image from your desktop into the dotted lined area. Once it's uploaded, the file will appear at the bottom of the screen; click "Edit" on the far right hand side of the screen, and in the new window, under the "Save" tab in the right hand column, highlight and copy the link in the "File URL" box. This link will now be included at your Feedburner account, which communicates to iTunes, along with your RSS feed, how your artwork will be displayed.

> Next, log in to your Feedburner dashboard, and click the "Optimize" tab near the top of the screen.

➤ On the left hand column, you'll see that a number of options are listed, and near the bottom you'll see "Feed Image Burner". Click this tab.

➤ In the "Image Source" box, click "Specify custom image URL" in the dropdown. Then in the box below it with the same name, enter the URL to the image file you uploaded to your Wordpress account. The next box down, labeled "Image Title", allows you to display whatever text you like, which will appear instead of the image if the podcast art cannot be loaded for any reason. Finally, in the "Link" box at the bottom, you can include a link back to your blog or website.

➤ Be sure to click "Save" at the bottom of the page; you should see a message next to the save button that says, "This service is active" if everything has been correctly enabled.

Granted, not everyone is a professional graphic designer, so it may be that you're now scratching your head wondering how in the world you're supposed to make the iTunes artwork you'll upload during this process. Even if you aren't a professional artist, with a little practice, you may surprise yourself at how well you'd do at creating a simple image with text for your podcast art.

To do this will require some kind of photo and image editing software. While **Photoshop** is a natural choice for more experienced web designers, it is also a relatively costly program, especially for anyone who doesn't plan to use it frequently. Alternatives include open-source programs like **Gimp** or **CinePaint**, as well as that time-tested classic, **Microsoft Paint** (anyone out there with some experience as a graphic designer may be cringing right now, but remember that the objective here is to provide a few options at low-cost for beginning podcasters). For Mac users, a nice place to meet in the middle is a program called **Pixelmator**, which is a very cost-effective alternative to Photoshop that can be purchased for just $29.99. I've used this program for years, and find that it is an excellent alternative that is both diverse and capable, despite not breaking the bank.

If you really feel that obtaining image editing software and starting from scratch is outside your comfort zone, there are programs that can assist you with creating the thumbnail graphic for your podcast. **Podcast Artwork Slicer** is a web-based program that requires no downloads, and will assist you with making artwork for your podcast for a flat-fee of $37. You can find them online at their website, www.podcastartworkslicer.com.

Finally, there's always the option of having someone create the artwork for you. Try seeing if you have any friends who would be willing to design your art to the technical specifications we covered earlier, and that way you can be involved with the design process, but without the hassle of going through a freelance website that requires creating an account, sorting through various bids by artists, and of course, working with a designer you've never met or worked with before.

I've also had fairly good experiences outsourcing small graphics jobs and other work I didn't have the time or skills to complete. This can be done using sites like www.Fiverr.com and www.Freelancer.com, among others. At least a small amount of money is going to be involved when you take "for hire" options like these, but doing so will often get you better results, and maybe even for less than the cost of purchasing one of the programs we mentioned earlier in the DIY section.

Making Art for Individual Episodes of Your Podcast

For many, the art you create for submission with your podcast RSS feed will be a one-time affair, in that once it's been created, uploaded to the web, and linked with your RSS feed, you'll never have to change it again (although you can, if you ever so desire, change your podcast art *any time you like*, simply by logging into your Feedburner account and following the steps we outlined earlier. Just remember that it may take a few days for any changes to be reflected in the iTunes store).

However, for those who want to go the extra mile in creating a quality podcast, something that might become a regular art-related project for you, should you choose to do it, is creating art for each individual episode of your podcast.

Why would you want to do this? Quite simply, making new art for each episode allows you to add an additional layer of customization; it's the simple difference between a blank audio file, and one that brings up a picture when you play it, which will no doubt help convey a greater sense of quality and professionalism.

A while back, I decided to do this, and though it may sound daunting to have to worry about the creation of new art for every episode, it's actually not as hard as it sounds, and it's certainly not as stringent as the process of creating iTunes artwork (or it doesn't have to be, at very least).

For the sake of clarity, I do want to make the distinction that the per-episode art we're discussing *is not* the same as the iTunes art you have created for your podcast; this is a smaller image file that you'll create with information specific to any single episode of your podcast, which is attached to the audio file itself, rather than to your podcast's feed.

Apart from those fundamental differences, this art can be created in much the same way that any other iTunes artwork is made. These files will be smaller than your iTunes art, as I've mentioned, with most podcasters featuring an image that's 300 by 300 pixels in size. This doesn't have to be elaborate either; you could literally use a solid colored background with the proper dimensions above, and with simple text (such as the podcast episode, date, number, season, or any other naming convention you choose for episodes of your show) appearing over it. But be careful: since this art will often be displayed in much smaller format than the art's actual dimensions, make sure the font sizes you pick are large enough that they can be read once the image has been reduced down to the size it will appear when users download the file.

Once you create this image file, adding it to the podcast episode can be done very simply. One of the easiest ways to do it is by using iTunes:

➢ Open iTunes on your computer, and drag to add the mp3 file of your podcast to your iTunes library

➢ Right click on the file in iTunes (or control click for Mac) and choose the "Get Info" option

➢ In the new window, click on the "Artwork" tab and add the image by dragging it into the space provided, then click "Okay"

While you're adding your artwork to the podcast file, you may also want to visit the "Details" tab and add information under the "Artist" headings, such as the name of your podcast, as well as the names of the hosts. This way, when the file is opened in a program like iTunes, it will also display things like the show's name, the episode title, and the talent featured in it along with the artwork you've created.

A final consideration, with the future of things in mind, is that as your podcast continues to grow, some of the same principles of art and design applied here, even in the very simplest ways, may later come in handy with regard to creating similar artwork for the website that hosts your podcast. There's no rule that says all of your art has to be identical across the various mediums on the web you'll utilize, but when it comes to branding your show with art that your listeners will recognize, it's not a bad idea to keep some degree of continuity in mind, whether it be the images, fonts, or other stylistic features you'll use with the images you create for your show.

Other Platforms For Bringing Your Podcast to the World

While much more could be said about additional sites and resources you may wish to use for your podcast, what we've outlined above addresses the simplest, and frankly the *best* way to accomplish your mission of getting a podcast together and making it available online. However, there are a few final pointers I'll address here that you may find useful as well. Primarily, these include alternatives to iTunes that you may wish to use for additional reach (so your podcast is made available in as many places on the web as possible), as well as a few helpful things to bear in mind about using services like YouTube.

Stitcher (www.stitcher.com) has become a popular podcast community, which, like iTunes, features a fairly basic submission process for its applicants. Once you've submitted your podcast's feed, you're generally approved within just a few days, and soon afterward a page is created where your podcast's episodes can be streamed or downloaded. While some view it as an "alternative" to iTunes, it is generally best to use sites like this *in addition to* iTunes, rather than as an exclusive alternative. Submit your feed to Stitcher here: http://stitcher.com/contentProviders.php

TuneIn (www.tunein.com) is a site advertised primarily as a medium for online radio that features both music and streaming talk stations, but there is accessibility for podcasters here just as well. As of the time this book was written, TuneIn advertises that they host more than four million on-demand programs through their services.

Other options include **Zune**, which many podcasters like using, as well as **Blackberry** (that's right, the same company that makes the phones). In truth, while some still use these podcast directories, I would still recommend keeping your focus with iTunes, Stitcher, and TuneIn.

There's always **YouTube** for consideration too, and while this one may seem fairly obvious by now, there are actually a lot of unique benefits to hosting your podcast on YouTube, in addition to other locations on the web. The biggest difference here is that, unlike podcast directories, YouTube doesn't utilize an RSS feed interface, but instead has each user create an account that they upload content to directly. While this involves a little more work, it also offers some unique perks worth considering.

For starters, YouTube allows you to pair visuals with the audio files you host, which may range from still images you feature in a video you create to accompany the podcast files you upload, to a live video broadcast of the show that you may create while recording. One way to implement this for live listenership is to use the free **Google Hangouts** app, a live video chatting system that can be launched from anyone's personal Google account. One of the most unique features it provides, called "Google Hangouts for Air", allows live streaming of your Google Hangout directly to your YouTube account, for which you can then obtain an embed code, and thus stream your live show to any website where you embed your YouTube player link.

I have used this feature to broadcast live shows from my website while also recording the podcast live. For those who prefer not to stream video along with their show, an image overlay option will allow you to stream audio accompanied only by a picture of your choosing, such as your podcast's logo (and I'll explain in detail how this can be done later in a section devoted to live streaming). Best of all, once the live stream is terminated, the show is then archived automatically, *and uploaded directly to your YouTube page.* How's that for hands free?

Keep in mind, of course, that unless you're comfortable doing your show in a live format, Google Hangouts may not be the best way to incorporate YouTube into what you're doing with your podcast (especially since many podcasters enjoy the luxury of being able to record their shows, and then go back to edit the file afterward). If you're a podcaster who follows Leo Laporte's "straight to air" kind of format, this option may work well for you, just as it has for me in the past. Another thing to keep in mind, however, is that the Google Hangouts app can be a bit unreliable and buggy at times, maybe partly as a result of the tremendous bandwidth strain of thousands of users around the world streaming their Hangouts live, and completely for free, at any given time. As we've discussed several times already, many free services like these are nothing short of remarkable, considering what you get out of them at virtually no cost; but they're still far from being perfect, and generally more costly paid-for options are the only way to go for serious professionals.

I've spoken to many podcasters over the years, and despite the accessibility and numbers they can achieve with their podcast downloads alone, many of them still swear by the amount of traffic their shows receive after they've been uploaded to YouTube. For those seeking to find ways of achieving maximum reach with their podcast, this is certainly an option that should be considered seriously, since the YouTube community allows your podcast to be discovered by the wide array of web surfers who haunt YouTube at every hour, using the site's search engine functionality to stumble onto various things they may not have been searching for consciously. Thus, keywords should be added to your uploaded videos, since they are just as important here as any Search Engine Optimization (SEO) you might employ with a website (and for the laymen out there, SEO is basically the use of key terms and coding to help search engines like Google find your site more easily when users search for your brand or related subjects your site may feature). With proper keywords implemented, as well as a consistent schedule for adding content, some podcasters I've spoken with actually claim that they get *more* traffic with YouTube than they do their regular podcast downloads; this is particularly useful for users who choose to run Google Ads on their YouTube videos, which can become profitable in the long run for those operating high-traffic video channels.

And of course, if you decide to use any of these (or other) services to host your podcast on the web, remember that an account with Auphonic.com will not only grant you access to audio processing services, but also the ability to upload your audio to several locations on the web *simultaneously*, which include sites like YouTube.

These are just a few final considerations within the realm of podcasting on the inexpensive side of things, and as the last few paragraphs have shown, some of these strategies could actually help you generate revenue in the long term as well, with little upfront costs associated. I would still emphasize that by spending at least enough to improve the quality of the content you provide, whether that's through buying microphones and equipment, or subscribing to hosting services that allow your audience to access your content more quickly and reliably, you will benefit greatly in the long run. You don't *have* to invest thousands of dollars to achieve the right balance between the quality you offer, and the goals you hope to achieve; whether those fall under monetary rewards, or purely the satisfaction of producing good podcasts for a large listener base.

Wherever you may stand with your long term goals as a podcaster, in this next section we're going to begin looking at ways you can build an arsenal of podcasting equipment that will put your sound and production on par with the very best in the business. The sky really is the limit here, and fortunately, even some of the best collections of gear available to serious podcasters aren't nearly as costly as other hobbies or businesses can often be. In addition to being relatively inexpensive, serious podcasting can also be a hell of a lot of fun; and yes, it can even become profitable.

CHAPTER THREE: GOING PRO

"The main foundations of every state, new states as well as ancient or composite ones, are good laws and good arms—you cannot have good laws without good arms, and where there are good arms, good laws inevitably follow."

Some of you may recognize these as the words of that famed, and equally controversial political philosopher, Niccolo Machiavelli. While they may appear irrelevant to the humble podcaster, their essence does apply to your objectives just as well: in the last chapter, I have taken great pains to present a set of "laws", in a sense, by presenting an order of operations for what, in my experience, has proven to be the most effective method of implementing a podcast. Up until now, however, we have looked at how this can be done on a very minimal budget; while many (most, in fact) of the things we've discussed will still apply to a more professional—and thus, at times more expensive— approach to podcasting, there are still new concepts that will have to be addressed, which include discussion of things like purchasing web server space and hosting your own website, as well as acquiring a hosting plan for your audio with unlimited bandwidth. And, of course, there is the necessity of purchasing good equipment to help ensure that your podcasts will sound their very best.

"Good arms," in other words, to help implement the "good laws" we've already examined, which we will build upon shortly.

While we're on the subject of philosophy, it is true that the concept of having the right tools for the job has inspired many a thinker who have come and gone. Chief among them, perhaps, had been Machiavelli, as we have seen here; which is why his practical (and sometimes disconcerting) attitude toward things became a small part of the intelligent mockery I have worked into my shows over the years. This includes a podcast I used to do called *Middle Theory*, and you can still find the episodes of this show archived at www.middletheory.com (as part of your homework, I do recommend that you go listen to this, of course).

But before we move on, let me offer you a less esoteric quote, where similar sentiments about the implements of warfare are equally well-stated, though perhaps with less elegance: "Hokey religions and ancient weapons are no match for a good blaster at your side, kid."

In that same spirit of Spartan simplicity, it's time we go get some frickin' blasters.

Game On: Purchasing Web Space and Building a Website

Up until now, everything we have talked about for your podcast, with the exception of equipment like microphones and mixers, utilizes resources that are freely available on the web. Even for those who will wish to get more out of their podcast by hosting a professional website and other paid services that will optimize the quality of your production, a majority of what we have covered already will still carry over. The differences will have mostly to do with the kinds of services you may choose, and the ways you may choose to implement them. For instance, I still recommend using Wordpress as the backbone of your website, since it is open-source software that is freely available, constantly being updated, and with the use of different themes and add-ons called **plugins**, it can be made to do just about anything you want in terms of how your website will look and function... without having to have a lot of knowledge of web programming and how to write code beforehand.

However, the difference between using a free Wordpress.com account for your site, and installing the program on a server you acquire, will be like night and day. In fact, many of the plugins we discuss in this book aren't even a feature available to users exclusive to Wordpress.com; you'll actually need to download and install a version on a web server before you can enable these powerful add-ons (although one of the most flexible Wordpress plugins, Jetpack, will require you to have a Wordpress.com account *in addition to* your installed version, so you can link your site to your Wordpress account and enable the plugin's features).

There are many reasons apart from tech considerations that justify having your own website. For starters, it gives you ultimate control over what you do, and how you'll do it. Of equal importance is the ability to have a professional public appearance, and nothing says that like having your own website, with its own specific URL, and a clean, professional, and functional layout and design. We've already addressed a lot of this earlier in the book, so I won't go into great depth right now about the philosophy of owning a website. We will, however, look at a few of the varieties of different approaches to securing web space and building a site that you may want to consider.

Before you can begin building a website you'll need a **web host**, which is the service that actually provides space on the Internet for websites.

According to Consumer-Rankings.com, "a product and service comparison website that rates and reviews the leading brands across select industries," the top ten web hosting services (as of 2015) in its rankings are as follows:

1. iPage.com,
2. Bluehost.com
3. HostGator.com
4. JustHost.com
5. Yahoo.com
6. Arvixe.com
7. IXWebHosting
8. GoDaddy.com
9. FatCow.com
10. NetworkSolutions.com

I will point out that I do not use any of these companies for my own websites, nor have I ever used any of those listed here. I have no particular prejudices against them either; it's simply a matter of having chosen a different company from those listed, which I'll tell you about shortly. However, in the past, one web host provider I worked with was owned by one of these companies, and that experience wasn't particularly a positive one.

The reason for this was simple: from time to time, even a web guru will need to be able to work with the tech support personnel employed by their web hosting company. There are occasionally issues that may arise on the "server side" of things which you'll need them to address, since you—a customer—can't be given access to the *entire* server, in the event that some broader-reaching problem occurs. Therefore, it is very important that your tech support personnel are up to snuff on how things like Wordpress, HTML and PHP coding, and other similar things actually work.

My problem had been with the tech support offered by this previous web host in just such an instance, where a problem originating from their servers had crippled the RSS feeds my sites were generating. The result was that my podcasts were not appearing on iTunes, or in any other places, as they were supposed to. I managed to diagnose what the problem was with the help of independent tech experts (one of whom I paid handsomely, I might add) only to find that the problem *still* couldn't be resolved without server-side support. Logically, I felt that if I explained this to the tech support staff, they would understand what the problem was, and fix it for me.

Boy, was I ever wrong. Initially, the level of skill and professionalism this company's tech support had offered had been very good at the outset, but over time it began to show a marked decline. In the midst of the problem I described above, the height of my frustration occurred when a tech support official advised that I had broken my own website "by upgrading to the latest version of Wordpress." I explained to this individual that *all* of my sites were affected, even those which hadn't been upgraded yet, to which they (or it... I'm still not entirely sure it was a human I was speaking with on this occasion) advised, "You should never upgrade if your Wordpress site is already working the way you like for it to."

This is complete and utter *rubbish*, because while occasionally there might be problems that arise from a Wordpress upgrade, these updates are designed to help prevent security problems that might arise from using out-of-date software on your site. My IT friends laughed at this when I told them about it, comparing their actions to making up idiotic "solutions" while not actually doing anything to solve the problem. After several subsequent verbal wrestling matches that only proved to me that I knew more than what was printed on the reference cards the folks at "tech support" had been taking their cues off of, I was finally sent to a senior staff member for assistance. He did precisely what I told him to do (as I had been told to tell him by my independent tech experts), and found that the issue was just as we had determined on our end of things. Despite finally correcting the issue, I was so frustrated by the lack of communication (and the money lost while trying to help tech support learn how to fix the problem) that I switched providers. I dropped them like a hot rock, and never looked back.

On a friend's recommendation (the friend was actually Gene Steinberg, host of a radio program called "The Tech Night Owl", which you can find at www.technightowl.com), I switched to a company called NameCheap.com, and have found that their service is some of the best I've worked with. My sites load more quickly and reliably, and yes, their tech support has never failed in helping address any problem I've had, though I've also had far fewer tech issues after switching. As an added bonus, their services even cost less than that of my previous providers.

So the point here that I would like to get across to you is simple: before you pick a web host, read reviews from others who use their services, and also do a Google search for ratings and reviews their tech support has received in recent months. Don't pick a web provider based solely on how inexpensive their services are, or on whether they offer simple templates that help you build a website, since what you'll likely be doing anyway is using an auto-install service they will offer (as most hosting providers do) to install a program like Wordpress automatically, and then troubleshooting any further issues with the reliable tech support of the company you've researched thoroughly before you bit the bullet and bought a plan.

There are a variety of different options in terms of the kind of hosting you will buy, which most providers will detail in different plans available on their websites. These generally involve **shared hosting**, where you purchase space on a server where other user accounts are hosted as well, or a more expensive option where you have your own **dedicated server** which is provided exclusively for your own use. There are other options that may be involved, such as what some companies call "virtual hosting," which simply means using a single server to host multiple different domain names. My simplest advice to you would be never to pick the least expensive option if you can afford not to do so, but unless you are planning to build a serious website for a new business startup, or otherwise plan to have a site that will demand a huge server load (such as one that will feature streaming audio or video content, like an online radio station), then you likely will not require having a fully dedicated server, which usually will cost you to the tune of a few hundred dollars a month. There are many reasonable hosting plans that will cost you a fraction of that, and usually for just a few dollars a month (though keep in mind, they'll advertise these low monthly prices on their website, but nearly always use an annual billing cycle. Just be aware of that when you sign up).

A final consideration with regard to purchasing a hosting plan is the actual domain you purchase. You will need to select a domain name that is either the same as, or at least close to, the name of the podcast you'll be using this website to represent. If the domain name you pick is already taken, you won't be allowed to make the purchase, in which case the next best option may be to look at whether the same name, but with ".org" or ".net" rather than ".com" is available. The hosting provider you've been looking at will also offer you the ability to purchase domains through their company, but some people prefer to go to a company such as **GoDaddy** or some similar site, where they can purchase their domain name for less, and then use the Domain Name Servers provided by the hosting company they work with to point that domain to their server. Whichever option you choose is up to you, although the simplest in this case is generally to buy your domain through the hosting company you choose, so that it will automatically be associated with the server space you purchase.

When it comes to building a website, you have a number of options available to you, but as I've discussed throughout this book, in the interest of time and space we will be looking at using Wordpress as the primary platform for your site. As mentioned, I have seldom found a web hosting company that didn't offer some kind of simple auto-install feature you can use to implement the latest version of Wordpress on your server, thanks in large part to the program's popularity in the last few years as a simple blogging template for websites. If you have questions about how this auto-install function may work with your hosting plan, just sign in to the account for the plan you purchase, and locate their tech support help line number, or wherever else you can submit a support ticket, and explain to them that you'd like Wordpress installed on your server. They will likely ask you for a few details, such as the user name and password you'll want, and then you'll receive an email shortly afterward with a link to where you can log in to your new Wordpress site.

If you already have a Wordpress.com account, you will have had time to familiarize yourself with some of the program's features. But even if you're new to Wordpress, its functionality is very simple to figure out, and any number of tutorials on how to install and use it can be found by visiting Wordpress.org.

A few things you *may not* be familiar with will be the expansive number of theme templates and plugins that will be accessible to you now, having the complete version of Wordpress on your server. **Themes** are different versions of predesigned site layouts you can download and install for your Wordpress site, which will combine different color schemes, arrangements of site elements (such as main content and sidebars using what Wordpress calls "widgets", which feature site components like calendars, images, and even embedded windows to your Twitter and Facebook accounts). Some professional themes are available for purchase through third party sites, but a vast number of comprehensive themes are made available for free by Wordpress as well.

When it comes to plugins, there are simply too many of them available to describe them all here. You can find plugins that will perform any number of functions you may want your site to have. These include optimized media players for your show, like the **Smart Podcast Player** designed by Pat Flynn (www.smartpodcastplayer.com), which is a paid-for plugin with an annual subscription rate (while it's a bit costly, arguably it's *well* worth the money, considering how well it works... never expect less than the best from Pat, period). But for now, all other options aside, there is one primary free plugin for podcasters that I feel it is important that you know about.

The **Blubrry PowerPress Podcasting plugin** is arguably the most popular podcasting plugin among Wordpress users today. This plugin will do many of the same things that we learned to do with Feedburner in Chapter Two, such as changing your iTunes podcast art. Some will still recommend that podcasters use Feedburner to generate the RSS feed you will actually submit to iTunes, because it remains the most reliable free way to change the input RSS feed that communicates to iTunes what your podcast's RSS feed source will be. Therefore, you can use Blubrry PowerPress and Feedburner's services together. However, I will note that the folks at Blubrry advise strongly against doing this, and in truth, using both services is not required. As I've outlined, all Feedburner really does is allow you to change your feed with less hassle, so long as the folks at Google continue to offer the service.

Blubrry PowerPress also features a host of configuration options, offers various statistics and reports, and it supports more than two-dozen podcasting file formats. In the latest version, a new feature for podcast SEO has also been added, to help make your podcast more visible on the World Wide Web.

Once Blubrry PowerPress is installed in Wordpress, you will see in the left hand column of your Wordpress Dashboard that "PowerPress" will have its own icon below the "Settings" tab. Clicking here will take you to the PowerPress dashboard, where you will be able to scroll through multiple tabs that incorporate a variety of settings and optimization modes for your podcast. The Default Mode is a basic primer that will have all the essentials for getting your podcast up and running with Wordpress, which includes a breakdown of how (and where) to submit your podcast to iTunes, and then integrate that into the PowerPress plugin. For users who want to get a bit more in-depth with how they use the plugin, a button at the top of the page offers the ability to switch between the simplified Default Mode, as well as a more comprehensive Advanced Mode. Another great thing about the plugin is that it will create a podcast-specific feed for your site, which will feature only the posts related to podcast episodes that you publish. This feed will look like this:

http://www.your-site.com/feed/podcast/

And of course, this can be entered into the "Original Feed" box that appears when you click the blue "Edit Feed Details" tag under the heading near the top of your Feedburner dashboard, which then sends the podcast-only content to iTunes.

Once your podcast has been configured in this plugin, getting the podcasts linked to the posts you create is simple. Below the content entry field on any individual "New Post" page you create in Wordpress, the Blubrry PowerPress entry field will also appear, in it's own area called "Podcast Episode." The first box in this area is labeled "Media URL", and you will copy the direct link to your audio file once you upload it to the web, and paste it here. Then click the "Verify URL" button to the right, and wait for the green notification that the URL has been verified (if it can't verify the file, or the operation times out, simply click the "Verify URL" button again, and repeat the process until the file can be verified properly). Once you complete the rest of the details for your post, you will finish up by clicking the blue "publish" button, just as you would with any other post on your site. When you view the published post, the podcast will be accessible in a media player (which appears based on where you designate for it to be in the Settings area on the PowerPress plugin dashboard). Publishing a post with a PowerPress media file in this way also communicates directly with iTunes via RSS feed, so that your latest podcast episode appears online as well. How easy is that?

Hopefully, you'll find that this is both simpler, and more efficient than the methods detailed in the last chapter, and while they do require a bit of investment, everything we've described in this chapter thus far could be completed in a single day, and will be far more efficient than any of the "free" methods we've described earlier. Notice, however, that the processes still haven't changed much, and that the biggest difference with having your own Wordpress installation on a hosting plan is the plugin accessibility you now have, which optimizes and simplifies the podcast publication process. (Try saying that three times fast.)

Still, when it comes to getting your audio files online, there are greater problems that can arise from using free options, namely the speed and reliability which listeners can expect as they go to download or stream your audio. Depending on the length of your show, as well as the file format and bit rate you choose for saving your files (which we'll talk about in the next section), your file sizes may be fairly large. This can cause their download time to take a while, especially if hosted on a free site like archive.org.

You might be thinking at this point that, "hey, if I've purchased web space for my site, why don't I just upload my files there?" It sounds like a simple solution, and in truth, it might actually work for a while. But the moment your podcast begins to build any sort of a decent following, and the few dozen listeners you have suddenly becomes a few hundred, then a few *thousand*, you'll quickly find that the "unlimited bandwidth" that most hosting companies say they provide is *anything but* unlimited. Worst case scenario, this could even lead to what your hosting provider would consider "bandwidth abuse," where they may temporarily suspend your website, or even terminate their agreement with you if the issue isn't resolved promptly (that may sound harsh, but stranger things have happened... and yes, it happened to me once, so you can take my word for it).

But before you throw in the towel in frustration, in the next section we'll look at a number of bandwidth-friendly options for podcasters that offer *truly* unlimited storage (actually, "unmetered" is the term for this). In fact some of the solutions we're about to examine might even offer an all-in-one alternative to paid-for podcasting that you'll find seriously worthy of consideration.

'Unmetered' is the Word: Why You Need an Audio Hosting Plan

As we've just gone over, there are two practical reasons that you'll want to look at securing an audio storage plan for your podcast files. One of them involves giving your listeners better, and faster, access to the content you provide, and the other is a protection against the kinds of bandwidth problems you may face if you choose to store your files on your own server.

As I alluded earlier, I learned this the hard way a few years ago, as a result of storing my audio files on the same server where I had bought my hosting plan. It only took my podcast gaining a following of a few hundred subscribers before I woke up one day to a nice barrage of emails, warning me that my site had been suspended due to "bandwidth abuse." Fortunately, several friends of mine in the podcasting community were quick to steer me in the direction of a handy, and also relatively inexpensive solution to this sudden, but avoidable, little nightmare.

LibSyn.com is a podcast hosting and publishing service, which also features a number of publishing tools, media hosting options and plans, RSS feeds for content, iTunes integration, and even the ability to create a simple Smartphone app for your show. Perhaps very best of all, each plan they offer features that fabled and long-sought "unmetered bandwidth" we've been discussing, which means there are no restrictions on the number of times your podcast can be downloaded each month, and

144

that includes both the latest episodes, as well as those in your archives.

The process is explained thusly on the "Features" page at the LibSyn website:

"Liberated Syndication pioneered the system of expanding storage for podcasting. We recognized early on that one of the most appealing aspects of the medium is the ability for the audience to go back through time and enjoy earlier episodes once they've discovered a show. Our studies have shown more than 50% of the monthly downloads a show receives is from its back catalogue of content. With libsyn, you don't need to worry about running out of space for your show."

With LibSyn's "expanding storage" system, podcasters are able to upload content on a schedule that fits their budget, and new space is added constantly in incremental amounts over time, in accordance with the allotments of the plan you have purchased. That means that once it's time for your next episode to be uploaded, new space has been made for that content, while your old content remains for as long as your account is active. To learn more about LibSyn, you can visit the following link: http://www.libsyn.com/features/. Also, LibSyn is well known for having very friendly and reliable support, so if you still have questions about their system and how it works, you can always use their "Contact" page to reach out.

Podcasters may use LibSyn and its features in a variety of ways, based on their individual needs, though most use it primarily for hosting audio, for which they will then obtain a link, and then post this to their website (conversely, some podcasters may opt to work exclusively with LibSyn's features for their podcast, and forgo using a website at all, as I'll discuss in a moment). Despite the variety of ways a podcaster can use LibSyn, the basic process goes something like this:

- ➢ Log in to your LibSyn account, and from the dashboard page, navigate to the "Content" tab, where there are different options for how you can add a new episode

- ➢ Upload your audio file to your LibSyn account

- ➢ Unless you are using the RSS feed LibSyn provides as your interface with iTunes or Feedburner, you will then obtain a direct URL to your audio file once the upload is complete, which is copied and pasted at your website in a location such as the "Media

URL" field using the Blubrry PowerPress
plugin

As you've already seen, LibSyn does provide its own RSS feed for your podcast, but that's not all. There is also a Libsyn Podcast Page, which along with the RSS feed, can be seen by visiting the "Destinations" tab on the LibSyn dashboard. The Podcast Page can actually serve as the site for your show if you so desire, using the accompanying RSS feed as the primary "input feed" for your podcast (which, as you can probably guess, will work fine with your Feedburner account, just like any other RSS feed you might care to burn through it). So in essence, some podcasters may find that using LibSyn's features will solve both the audio hosting dilemma, as well as the website issue as well.

While this is all very true, I should emphasize that you will without question get the most freedom, flexibility, and overall professional appearance from the creation of a standalone website, which serves as the online presence for your podcast. I can't think of one serious podcast that doesn't implement this basic approach of having a website, and a podcast they submit to iTunes, for which audio files are stored through LibSyn or some similar audio hosting service.

LibSyn offers a number of pricing options for podcasters as well, starting with plans as cheap as $5 per month. There are a number of factors that may influence the plan you'll want to purchase (which are billed monthly, rather than annually like most web hosting plans), based on your storage space needs. These factors include how often you will post your shows, and what their file size and format will be, since LibSyn storage plans add new space on an incremental basis, as described earlier. Generally, in my experience a plan in the $15 to $30 monthly range will work for the needs of most podcasters, presuming that you'll have a podcast that features episodes that are between one and two hours in length, and with an episode frequency of maybe one or two shows posted weekly. That said, the actual *physical size* of the audio files you'll be uploading will present you with an equal space consideration, so with that in mind, we'll quickly look at LibSyn's guidelines and recommendations for creating audio files for storage:

> ➢ The MP3 file format is the gold standard of podcasting. While some people may prefer to use higher quality file formats, generally the human ear can't easily distinguish between a high quality MP3 recording and a WAV or AAC file (at least when most of the

audio file features the human voice in a spoken-word format, rather than music, as is the case with podcasts). However, LibSyn warns that they, "do not recommend using AAC (M4A) files as they will not play on Blackberry devices and many other portable media players."

➢ The recommended Stereo Bit Rate for spoken word shows is 192 kbps, but LibSyn suggests using the Mono Channel unless the show features lots of music (when Channels are set to Mono, the above figure gets cut in half). A sample rate of 44.1 kHz is the standard for this (a quick hint: I almost always bounce my podcast audio files down to mono format, as this will not only save space, but *most* of your listeners will not notice the difference if, again, the majority of your show is spoken word).

➢ Programming featuring mostly music should be recorded at a Stereo Bit Rate of 128 kbps, and also at 44.1 kHz (Channels remain in the Stereo configuration, and the Stereo Mode in Joint Stereo).

➤ Finally, LibSyn warns (and they're serious, let me tell you), about **never** saving your files to a Variable Bit Rate. "You want your MP3 files to be CBR (Constant Bit Rate)," and I'd advise you take their word for it.

Finally, when it comes to saving your files in an MP3 format, some recording programs don't make it particularly easy to do this. If you ever find yourself in this predicament, the simplest way to get around the problem is to let iTunes do it for you. Here's a rundown of how to do that:

➤ Navigate to the "Preferences" tab in iTunes by either going to the "iTunes" tab in the toolbar on Mac, or under "File" for PC users.

➤ In the "Preferences" area, next you'll select "General", and then "Importing Settings"

➤ A new window should pop up, where you will see a field that reads "Import Using". Set this to "MP3 Encoder"

➤ Next, in the "Settings" field, change it to "Custom"

➢ Finally, in the new window that appears, you can customize settings to reflect those based on the specifications you choose, such as those outlined by LibSyn at their website. Click "Ok" in all the prompts that appear afterward to save your changes.

You'll see from the information we've covered in the last few paragraphs that LibSyn provides an extremely comprehensive service, with a multitude of features that have placed them high among the ranks of podcaster favorites. One thing that we haven't mentioned yet is that they also present podcasters with options for monetizing their podcasts, which generally involve a revenue share with LibSyn on earnings for subscriber only content, as well as some advertising options.

As always, there are still other options, and so in an effort to be thorough, here are a few more alternatives you might consider:

➢ **Blubrry**: That's right, remember the fine folks who made that hip little plugin you're using on your Wordpress site? They also offer file storage services, which like their plugin, is integrated through Wordpress (some feel this actually makes their interface a bit easier to use than LibSyn). Blubrry also has options for listing programs on mediums like Roku, Boxee, Samsung SmartTV, Lookee TV, and other devices. You can learn more here: http://create.blubrry.com/resources/podcast-media-hosting/

➢ **Amazon S3**: This is another option, but if you recall the situation we described in Chapter One related by David Jackson from School of Podcasting (www.schoolofpodcasting.com), there are several issues involving costly fees that might arise from Amazon's "pay as you go" system, especially as your podcast grows in popularity.

➢ **Podbean:** Jackson once again gives us his expert opinion in the form of qualms he had with this service: he points out that they don't allow you to promote third-party items on your podcasts, and more simply, unlike LibSyn or Blubrry, Jackson says he had trouble finding "who runs the company, or where they are located."

If you're serious enough about your future as a podcaster that you're giving consideration to any of the suggested services we've outlined, then it's very important that I offer a fundamental truism before you go one step further: while these features, if properly implemented, will help you build a web presence with potential for professionalism in both appearance and functionality, *none of it* will amount to a hill of beans if you don't invest in decent audio equipment to match it.

That's why, if you're serious about taking up arms to join in the podcasting revolution, it's time we take a look at the "big guns" you'll need for the job: microphones, mixers, and other professional audio equipment that will help you build a home studio with enough bells and whistles to raise your neighbor's eyebrows, scare your little niece and nephew, and yes, even attract the attention of the military.

Maybe not that last one, but I can still guarantee that you'll definitely feel like a real mad scientist (and maybe look like one too; just reference my picture on the back cover) once you're surrounded with the kinds of toys we're about to look at.

It's time to pay a little visit the war room.

The War Room: Building Your Podcast Recording Studio

Arguably, more than headphones, or even those groovy little RSS icons you see all over the web, there is no symbol that better conveys the essence of podcasting than the microphone. That's because recording your voice with a microphone and then making that recording available online for anyone to download at his or her leisure is the fundamental premise behind the podcasting revolution. Granted, you'll still need headphones for the job, and as we're about to see, there are plenty of other good pieces of equipment you'll need if you're really going to take your podcasting to the professional level.

As a brief aside, I should clarify that, yes, there is such a thing as "professional podcasting," although sadly, I still sometimes encounter attitudes among my friends in the radio industry where podcasting is viewed as being merely "poor man's radio." In their minds, podcasting is something that's just for "amateurs", and that real commentators don't have to hide behind their edits, and should be able to do with live radio what they do on any recording, if it's going to be worth listening to. While I strongly disagree with this attitude, I get around it myself by streaming my podcast live, for free, *while it's being recorded*, after which very few edits are usually ever done. But then again, I also have a background in broadcast radio; not everyone else does, and I therefore realize that not everyone is going to feel as comfortable "going live" as I do.

This is one of the main reasons I support podcasting so strongly: because it provides a voice to individuals within their own comfort and ability range. Call that "amateur" if you want, but I'd argue with anyone who thinks that the listen-on-demand format hasn't affected the way people consume media. Even popular live radio shows these days often have as wide a listenership (if not wider) with the recordings of their broadcasts that they upload to the web after their shows, simply because it grants people the convenience of being able to listen to that show any time they want, at any time that is best for them. Even the big names in talk radio are still relying on the podcasting medium, and perhaps every bit as heavily as those who never broadcast their shows to a live audience.

When using the right tools, I argue that it is not only possible for podcasters to match the sounds of professional, syndicated talk radio shows, but also in some cases you may produce audio that is actually more creative and engaging, as well as having better quality overall. To achieve this, you'll want to be sure what you're giving your audience sounds worth a hoot, so we'll look at the equipment you'll need for this in a moment.

But before we do that, let me say that if you're going to go to the trouble of buying good equipment for your podcasting arsenal, there are a few simple things you should consider beforehand.

First, professional podcasting is not about *how much* equipment you have; it has everything to do with the quality of what you produce, and that does often rely on the quality of the equipment you own. Ten to one, you will be better off with three or four quality pieces of gear than you would be using a mountain of inexpensive junk. But even with that in mind, at the end of the day *nothing* will be able to replace your natural abilities as a podcaster, and that relies almost solely on your personality, your voice, your knowledge, and how all of these things combine and work harmoniously when you sit in front of a microphone. Don't let people give you grief about what you're using, or how little you have, and why *they think* you'd be better off using this or that. You don't have to be that kid in the neighborhood with all the newest toys; just find the best quality equipment within your budget, and begin by purchasing only the essentials you need to create a podcast. I always recommend buying no more than what you absolutely require in the beginning, and then add more as you gain experience, or as you want to try incorporating new things into what you do. If your studio eventually ends up looking like the main deck of the Starship Enterprise, and you like it that way, then go for it;

but you can still have a great podcasting studio in a space no bigger than a walk-in closet.

Following this logic, in the next section we will primarily be looking at microphones, mixers, and headphones, along with a few other accessories that will be integral to the studio you're about to build.

Get On the Mic: Choosing the Right Microphone for the Job

While I maintain that less is often more, I do also advise that you not be strictly Spartan in your approach. When it comes to picking a microphone, a lot of podcasters can get the entire job done with a USB mic and a laptop, as we described earlier in this book. But when it comes to professional podcasting, I am of the opinion that you really will need a bit more than this, and here's why.

When you plug your microphone straight into your computer, what you're doing is creating a direct line between your mouth and your recording interface. Once you've recorded something, you can always use editing programs to change the sound of that, but if you want to be as efficient as possible with your podcasting, you will want to eliminate as much post-production work as you can. One way to help ensure this is to optimize the signal as it's *going in*, so that what you record sounds great *before* you begin editing.

This is why I would advise you to forget about USB microphones for your podcasting studio at home (although they can be great to have for traveling, so you can still podcast while on the move). Cliff Ravenscraft, who you'll remember me mentioning earlier in the book, advises: "One major reason is that it limits you to recording straight into your computer. I find there are a number of issues with recording into your computer directly."

As we talked about before, Cliff suggests that you record your shows into an external audio recorder, so that if anything bizarre happens with your computer while you're recording, you won't lose all of your work. USB microphones that plug directly into a computer can make it difficult to capture the audio from an external source in this way. Once again, I can't tell you how many times I've had a PC badly in need of defragmenting (which can happen fairly regularly if you're using that computer for recording audio) that froze up in the middle of a recording session. What Cliff recommends is by far the safest solution, but if you're not going to use an external recorder, at least try to stop fairly often, and save your work, just to be on the safe side.

I'm sure another reason Cliff makes this recommendation is because, coming back to what I said about optimizing the sounds going into your recording interface, a USB microphone prevents you from being able to use a mixer to add or remove low, mid, or high-end frequencies, in addition to having the option of incorporating multiple channels of audio recorded live to a single source (which we'll discuss later in the section about mixers). So the bottom line here is to put those USB microphones out of your mind, for now.

Another question about microphones that often arises is whether to use dynamic microphones or condensers. While I have owned many condensers that have sounded great, one thing about them is that they tend to pick up a lot of "room noise", which means sounds that are more than just a few inches away from the microphone can still be heard easily while using them. That's why, both in podcasting and with radio broadcasts, a lot of professionals will tell you to use a dynamic microphone. These microphones feature "close pattern" functionality that generally only picks up sounds within a few inches of the mouthpiece, which will greatly cut down on excess noise while you're recording (especially if you have co-hosts in the same room with you).

The go-to microphone among podcasters these days is the **Heil PR-40**, a favorite cited by the likes of tech-expert Leo Laporte, as well as late-night radio maestro Art Bell. What's great about this microphone is that, despite being a favorite among pros, it is relatively inexpensive; you can often purchase these online for a little under $350. Or, if you'd like to get one in a bundle with bells and whistles like a boom arm or a pop filter, Cliff Ravenscraft offers Heil PR-40 packages at his website: http://podcastanswerman.com/equipment/

Another industry standard that you will often see in big-time radio studios is the **Electro Voice R-20**. This microphone truly is the industry standard, and you will seldom enter any professional broadcast facility that isn't adorned with several of these. They are slightly more expensive than the PR-40, however, at around $450 (although I do see used models selling frequently online that make them comparable to the PR-40 in price). For those who like the look and feel of the EV R-20 but can't justify the price, they also offer a slightly less expensive model called the **EV RE320**, which clocks in at about the same price as you might see a used PR-40 running on sites like Amazon.com.

Another mic that's popular both for podcasting and broadcast is the **Shure SM-7B**, which is priced about the same as the Heil PR-40. This microphone has been a popular choice especially for studio use, both for recording vocals in a musical setting, as well as for broadcast radio and podcasting.

The **Sennheiser MD 421 II** is another dynamic mic that many swear by, which again is comparable in price to the Heil PR-40. I maintain that you don't have to spend quite this much if you want a decent sound, though. One microphone I've used for years (although it is a bit cumbersome in size) is the **MXL V900**, which is actually a large diaphragm condenser microphone with an internal shock-mount and pop filter, cased within a great big retro-looking custom grill, similar to what you'd expect to see in old movies or vintage pictures from recording studios. This microphone can be found online for around $200, and offers remarkably good audio quality, but keep in mind that it, like most any condenser mic, will require phantom power to operate.

Another microphone made by the folks at MXL that's worth considering is the **MXL BCD-1**. This little microphone is a low-end, but quality option for podcasting and broadcast, and while you might not expect to find these in the studios of all the big time podcasting pros, they are an option that I have recommended more than once to beginning podcasters that are serious enough about sounding good, but still working on a tight budget (this model runs for as low as $170 through most online retailers).

Finally, while this microphone is by no means my first recommendation (hence why I've listed it last), the **MXL 990** is a condenser microphone that would work okay if you will be operating in a quiet room by yourself, though I have found room noise can still be a bit of a problem with these. They usually run for about $99 online, but I have periodically found sales and promotions where they will sometimes sell for as little as $50.

I can tell you in honesty that I have worked with every one of the microphones I have listed here, and the order in which I have listed them is generally reflective of their rank in terms of what I consider to be quality, reliability, and also cost considerations.

Mix It Up! Adding A Mixer to Optimize Sound and Flexibility

Arguably, the microphone you use for your podcasts will be among the most important pieces of equipment that you will buy. But to really achieve optimum control over how your voice sounds with the mic you choose, it will help to have some equipment that will process that signal by adding equalization, compression, and other effects that will give your voice a bit of extra *oomph*.

On a semantic note, remember that this term, "oomph", dates back to the 1930s in English usage, and literally means:

"The quality of being exciting, energetic, or sexually attractive"

These are all qualities you will want to be able to convey with your voice, so be sure and pay attention as we go over the options for mixers and, later, other processing equipment you'll eventually want to add to your arsenal.

One of the most popular choices for mixers you'll see these days is the **Behringer Xenyx 502**, which we discussed earlier in this book. There are pros and cons with this model (as with anything really), so first the good stuff: this unit is compact, and hence can be easily moved, and won't take up much space. It has basic controls for high, mid, and low frequencies, as well as gain knobs that allow various adjustments that will boost or tonally enhance your signal. It's also one of the least expensive mixers you can buy that will still achieve good quality audio, and there are a number of pros in the podcasting world that use them. For instance, Pat Flynn of *The Smart Passive Income Podcast* has used this model in the past, and Christopher McCollum, my co-host on the *Middle Theory* podcast (or "McNonymous", as he went by on the show) also used this board. Under optimum Skype calling conditions, we can easily make him sound like he's in the same room with me as we record our show over Skype, despite being across the country from each other.

On the down side, this little mixer with its simple, four-channel interface will limit the amount of audio inputs at your disposal. This means that if you have a fairly audio-rich show you're doing, you may have to add more elements in post-production, rather than cueing them up "live" (remember that even if you aren't doing a live broadcast of your program, it is still helpful to be able to fire audio from different sound sources, such as iTunes or another audio player, while you're actually doing the show... hence what I mean when I say "live" in this context). Another down side is that this mixer, while generally capable of good audio quality, is still on the lower end of the quality spectrum, and may begin to experience minor problems with audio quality over time as a result of use and general wear that incurs.

A model I would recommend over the Xenyx 502 is Behringer's **Xenyx 1202**, which will give you more channels, and a slightly more solid configuration for a little less than double the cost of the 502. However, another mixer I have used in the past that is preferable to either of these, and one of the most popular mixers among professional podcasters, is the **Xenyx 1204USB** and its sister model the **Xenyx 1204FX**. The 1204USB, as you might have guessed, features a USB interface that allows you to connect your mixer directly to your computer (however, it also features a variety of outputs that are equally suited for running your mixer into your computer using an analog configuration with 1/8 inch cables, like I often do). It also has a more robust design, and what's more, each of the four primary mic input channels features its own compression and secondary gain knobs, which allow you to dial in an impressive range of sounds for a console that costs only about $159.99. The 1204FX is essentially the same board, but with a digital FX chain included that can be used to create various sound effects such as echo, reverb, and several others.

I have owned one of the 1204USB models for years, and have used it in everything from podcasting and live radio formats, to live stage performance and simple recording. For the money, it is certainly a good option to consider.

Cliff Ravenscraft recommends a slightly different model of mixer that, for anyone whose goal is to spend a little more, but to get equipment that will get them optimal results and flexibility, is well worth the investment. The **Mackie 1402-VLZ4** is a mixer that features six three-pin mic inputs (rather than the four you'll find on the Behringer 1204 models), along with several additional audio inputs, each with a full range of controls. With this board, available for around $400 online, you will have no problem finding room on your mixer for multiple in-studio co-hosts, as well as guests, and audio sources for things such as phone lines or Skype, audio playback, and any number of other things.

Currently, I am using a different Mackie mixer than this, which is the **Mackie ProFX12**. Some time ago, I had an opportunity to work with this board during a podcasting consultation job I was hired for, and found it to be a remarkably good sounding unit, costing a little less than the 1402-VLZ4.

I should note that the latest model in this series, the **Mackie ProFX12v2**, costs around $279.99 through most online retailers. The differences between version one and version two are that the colors on the knobs have changed, switching from red, blue, and orange to neon versions of blue, green, and yellow. In my opinion, the color change wasn't much of an improvement, but their practical purpose likely was crafted with this mixer's functionality in low-light situations kept in mind (such as live performances in clubs, etc). Hence, the new colors might indeed work better for that. Also, the knobs on the faders are a little different, but again, someone must have thought it was an improvement, and perhaps worthy of a minor price increase from the previous design. Still, the new model is $120 less expensive than the 1402-VLZ4, and either version discussed here will offer you an altogether great sounding mixer.

Another thing to consider here is that unlike the Behringer 1204 models, the Mackie models we're discussing have no built-in compression controls. However, anyone interested in purchasing one of these Mackie boards would have little problem getting around this by incorporating an external compressor into their setup, which in the long run will sound far better anyway. These Mackie units do feature channel inserts (unlike the less expensive Behringer models) that allow compression from a separate unit to be added using a stereo cable, a process we'll discuss more later on. We will also look at some compressors that come recommended by a number of podcasters, along with a few points on how to implement them effectively, later in this chapter. I'll also include a brief section on how to dial in your mixer, and ways to get optimal sounds with your podcasting setup.

I'm All Ears: Selecting the Right Pair of Headphones for the Job

If you think that you can run out and buy just any old pair of headphones for your podcasting studio, then you're probably right: you really don't *have* to go and spend $200 on a pair of headphones just to be able to produce a quality podcast (especially since you're the only person who will be hearing anything through them).

What isn't a joke, however, is the fact that a pair of quality headphones will allow you a much better ability both to appreciate, as well as *improve* the sounds you're capable of producing. Hence, your abilities as a podcaster might actually improve also, simply by having a great set of cans (and I should clarify... "cans" is slang for headphones, although in some regions the same term might be used for toilets. We don't want anyone thinking that placing his or her head near various toiletry will help them improve their podcasts... talk about a crappy idea).

If you're already an audiophile going into this, one of the first things I recommend for podcasting is simply using what you've got on hand. But even if you aren't someone who has high-quality headphones lying around, the same might still apply. A solution—while it is by no means the best option—would be to try using the little ear buds you may have received with any Smartphone you've purchased. On occasion, I have found that these will offer fairly good results for podcasting, depending on the model in question (the ear buds that come with newer models of Apple's iPhone can produce a surprisingly satisfying dynamic range, for instance).

If you're like me though, and you're a bit more serious about the kinds of headgear you'll be using in your studio, then you may want to consider one of the following options.

There are three varieties of headphones I want to cover here, each made by Sony, that offer some of the best audio quality for in-studio use. Along with quality and cost-effective options, I always like to err to the judgment of experts if I can, in addition to telling you what things have worked for me personally, so you'll have a few options to choose from.

The first pair of headphones we'll look at here are **the Sony MDR V6**, which is the set I currently use. I must say that these have some of the most pristine audio quality of any set of headphones I've ever worked with. I do find that they can tend to accentuate high frequencies a bit more than other headphones, but this actually lends to the range of overall clarity they offer. Looking elsewhere, if anybody would know good headphones, you might have guessed it would be Cliff Ravenscraft, who offers a similar variety, the **Sony MDR 7506**, through his website. The biggest differences between these two models, apart from their overall appearance, is that the MDR V6's I use have a vintage style "coiled" cable that is a little more than three feet long, but which can extend to as much as 10 feet if needed. The MDR 7506's are also a little less expensive than the ones I prefer, but only by a few dollars.

Previously, the headphones I had been using were the **Sony MDRV200** models, which run for around $50, but that's if you can find them, as they appear increasingly difficult to locate online these days (not entirely impossible, though). In truth, these headphones have a much "muddier" sound overall when compared with the models above, and apart from the fact that they accentuate bass frequencies better than the average set of inexpensive headphones, nowadays I would almost prefer wearing a decent pair of ear buds as opposed to sporting these guys, if I had to choose.

I maintain that you'll want a good pair of headphones to go with your podcasting gear, since you'll want to be able to have a good idea about what your show actually sounds like when others download and listen to it. But this makes for another good point of advice I'll offer: everyone's ears interpret things a little differently, and some people are just going to prefer the sounds of certain mixes rather than others. In the past, I've had audio engineers listen to shows I produce, and largely compliment the production quality (I suppose it helps that I'm a musician also, and having worked some as a session guitarist and record producer over the years, having a good "ear for the mix" is a must above all others).

Early on, I would find that one or two very discerning listeners felt the low-end frequencies on some of my shows had been a bit heavy, which only became apparent on a loud sound system that accentuated those frequencies. To help "tune in" my audio so it sounded good across a variety of listening mediums, I tried out an old trick from my days of music production, where my fellow producers and I would take a mix that we liked the sound of with our headphones or studio monitors, and then go listen to that on the stereo system in one of our cars. Then we would play the same audio recording on another car stereo, comparing them back-to-back, and listen for any differences. You could even take this a bit further and try listening with different sets of headphones, on computer monitors, and in a variety of other settings to see where certain elements of your show might be improved. While a podcast will be nowhere near as labor intensive as professional music production and mastering, I find that many of these techniques will be helpful nonetheless, and you might try them out early on in your podcasting career; but at the end of the day, your money will often still be on the quality of the headphones you're using.

Since we're on the subject of headphones, and also since we've covered microphones previously, there is one area where the two converge, which seems like a brilliant catchall for many would-be podcasters. That involves a **microphone headset**, which allows you to don a pair of headphones that have a little microphone mounted on them, so you can work hands-free... and also look like a dork.

There are actually some quality headsets out there, but to me, part of the fun of podcasting is having a decent radio-style setup with a quality microphone, headphones, and other equipment. Being honest (as I have strived to do throughout this book), it is *very seldom* that I ever hear anyone using a headset that I think actually sounds good. In fact, more often than not, I think they sound *really bad*.

To illustrate this further, on one occasion I had been asked to help coach a gentleman who was going to be producing a podcast for a company he worked with. We went to great pains looking at equipment together, and I helped him find the proper gear for a good, reliable podcasting setup.

After a bit of planning and coaching, the moment came for him to record his first show, and despite a few minor hurdles, everything sounded fairly good. Hence, I thought I could now rest easy, having instructed another up-and-coming podcaster on the ways of bringing his voice to the world of recording.

Then, once again, all hell broke loose.

For his second show, he decided that all the podcasting gear we had bought was just too much to worry with, and so he switched to plugging a headset directly into his computer instead. Sure, it was easier to use; but the annoying hum and harsh high end frequencies that prevailed throughout the show nearly cancelled out the voice of his guest, calling in on a bad phone line that *still* may have sounded better than the $20 headset that was making the host's voice sound like it was being recorded with an 8-track recorder, in an empty coffee can somewhere on the dark side of the moon.

This, needless to say, ended up being his last show before the company replaced him with a new host... and a guy who would agree to use the right equipment for the job. The moral of this story: unless you're willing to shell out and get quality gear, you are far better off penny pinching with microphones and mixers, rather than cheap headsets when it comes to podcasting.

Odds & Ends: Supplemental Gear For Your Podcasting Studio

Fitted with a good microphone, a mixer to allow you control over individual volume levels and other aspects of your recording setup, and a quality set of headphones, you should now have the basic elements needed for your podcasting setup; that is, when paired with a decent computer, recording software, and some of the kinds of programs I covered earlier in Chapter One that are used for connecting with guests, audio playback, and other things.

In addition to these elements, you'll also need a basic assortment of audio cables, adapters, and other gear for connecting your equipment together. For instance, basic "three-pin" **XLR connector plugs,** otherwise called mic cables, will allow your microphone to connect with your mixing board, and if your mixer is a USB model, it should come equipped with a USB cable that will allow you to run that into your recording computer. Conversely, you may choose to connect your mixer to your computer using one of its audio outputs, to run something like a microphone cable or a 1/8-inch stereo cable directly into your computer. Or, for optimum sound, you might run this cable into an audio interface like the **Tascam US-144 MKII USB 2.0**, a device I've used for a number of years as the medium for sending audio from my board into my computer. Alternatively, if you've decided to go with an external recorder like the **Roland R-05 Digital Recorder** or the **Sony PCM-M10**, you would use one of the various outputs located on your mixing board to send a signal to this device in the same way, either using one or more microphone cables or stereo cables.

A general guide for cables you'll want to keep on hand is as follows, consisting of six basic types:

➤ **XLR cables**: These are for connecting microphones to your equipment, as well as for connecting various other audio devices. I recommend having at least four of these, but having between six and twelve lying around is a good idea.

➤ **Phone connectors**: Don't let the name fool you, since these are cables used to connect everything from electric guitars to their high-wattage amplifiers, to various equipment you'll want to have around your studio. Again, having between four and twelve or so would serve you well. There are two varieties you'll be concerned with; the larger 6.35 mm (1/4 inch) and 3.5 mm (1/8 inch) types, with mono and stereo varieties of each that are available. A helpful hint: one way to have the best of both worlds is to purchase 3.5 mm cables, for which 6.35 mm adapters can be used on either (or both) ends to create a variety of connectivity combinations. I have used all of the aforementioned combinations at one time or another.

➤ **XLR to phone connectors:** As the name implies, this is a hybrid that features an XLR connector on one end, and a phone connector on the other. There are varieties that feature both "male" and "female" XLR ends, which are essentially connectors that feature either protruding pins, or holes for receiving them respectively (quit laughing, this isn't a high school sex ed class here, ya runts).

➤ **RCA connectors:** Finally, these are the famous red and white cables you often see, used to connect various audio equipment in stereo configurations. Another subset within this category is a cable that combines RCA outputs on one end with a stereo 6.35 or 3.5 mm phone connector on the opposite end, much like the XLR to phone connectors above; try to keep at least two or three of each variety on hand in your studio.

There are still other varieties you may want to consider as well, such as various adapters, charging cables, USB cables, CAT-6 network cables, and a few others you still may employ in the most esoteric of situations (I've made it a habit to keep all the cables that come with any electronic devices I buy, even if I have numerous identical cables already, just to have plenty of junk on hand in case I ever suddenly need to create a new way of getting audio from one place to another in a pinch). But for general podcasting purposes, these which I have outlined for you here will get most jobs done for you, especially if you're combining cable varieties with adapter plugs, as described in the section above on phone connectors.

When it comes to having multiple co-hosts in the same studio, another thing you will want to invest in is a **headphone distribution amplifier**, which will take a stereo signal and split it into multiple outputs, so that several (usually four) sets of headphones can monitor the audio output coming from a single mixing board. An inexpensive, but reliable solution to this is the **Behringer HA400**, which is a simple unit that won't cost you more than about $25. However, more expensive models like the **Behringer HA4700** and the **PreSonus HP4** will allow a more diverse ability for users to adjust the settings on their individual audio channels, despite originating from the same source. Headphone distribution amps generally work by sending the signal from the "headphone out" jack on your mixer to the input on your distribution amp using a stereo audio cable. Users then will plug their headphones into any of the audio outputs on the amp, and adjust the settings according to their volume and tonal preferences.

Next up on our survey of supplemental gear is the **compressor**, which is a device we have already touched on earlier, since a few inexpensive mixers on the market feature basic, built-in compression controls. Defined roughly, a compressor is an electrical amplifier that reduces louder sounds, and increases quiet ones, by narrowing the dynamic range of an audio signal. To the human ear, when an audio signal featuring a person's voice is run through a compressor, it "fattens up" the signal, giving it the tonal body and strength it wouldn't normally have.

Arguably, one of the most popular models used by podcasters today is the **Behringer MDX-4600 Compressor/Limiter/Gate**. As its name implies, this device not only adds compression to an audio signal, but also a limiter (which is just another form of dynamic range compression) and a noise gate feature, which will help eliminate any noise that is below a certain frequency level (these are most useful in radio and podcasting for eliminating noise, such as audible hiss either from a microphone, or an audio signal). Another model of compressor I have used in the past, and which I still own, is the **DBX 160A**. While the Behringer model described above is really the best bang for the buck (and since it features the multiple different processing options I've already outlined), I certainly recommend this one for most podcasters. However, if you're really of a mind to add an element of powerful compression to your audio processing, the DBX 160A, while more expensive (this model generally runs for a little more than $400) is one of the best in the business. Keep in mind however, that the DBX is a single-channel compressor/limiter, while the Behringer MDX-4600 can accommodate up to four separate channels.

Another element that can be helpful for use is a **De-esser**, which does precisely what it sounds like it would do: it removes the often overbearing or characteristically intense "s" sounds of the human voice, along with other sibilant consonants like "z", or when a person goes "shhh!" or "psst." A less expensive model in the DBX catalogue that combines the best elements of the processing qualities we've described previously, along with the de-essing function, is the **DBX 286s**, which is only slightly more expensive than the Behringer MDX-4600. However, like the 160A, each of the DBX models outlined here are single channel units, and if your aim is to be able to route multiple audio sources through a single unit, Behringer's model is probably still the best device that combines multi-channel use with cost-effectiveness. Also, a de-essing effect can be achieved more simply by rolling back the high end (treble) frequency knob a bit on the channel in question on your mixing board.

Those with excess money to toss around might also incorporate **Multiband Equalizers** and other gear into their setups, but while there are obvious benefits to incorporating such high-dollar signal processing into the audio you produce, one thing to bear in mind about podcasting is that, generally, you will be saving your audio to formats that will be somewhat "lossy", since the objective of podcasting is to offer audio quality that is good enough in terms of podcasting audio standards, but also with things like storage space considerations kept in mind. I know very few podcasters who incorporate extremely elaborate setups into what they do, and usually their gear won't go much further than their microphones, mixers, headphones and distribution amps, and a multi-channel processor like the

Behringer MDX-4600. Anything else beyond that usually involves computers, a telephone hybrid (for taking phone calls, as we'll discuss later), or some similar piece of equipment. Again, the sky is the limit with what you can do to improve the sounds you achieve; but while the sky is awesome, a lot can be done without having to leave the ground, just as well.

Getting a Good Deal: Where to Buy Your Audio Equipment

If you're like me (which means you're like most of us), you'll want to get the best prices you can on the equipment you buy. In order to do that, part of what you must become a master of is looking for bargains while shopping. While you might think it requires some kind of a "sixth sense" to be able to find deals like this, there are really just a few things you'll want to keep in mind to get the best values for the gear you purchase.

For starters, ten to one, you will do better by shopping online. You will nearly always find better prices through online shopping, and when it comes to buying audio gear, it's very easy to find sites that will offer you free shipping with your purchase. A couple of my favorites are www.Sweetwater.com, as well as www.MusiciansFriend.com, which both offer untold amounts of equipment for the serious audio recording enthusiast. You can also find lots of good deals on www.Amazon.com (although that one's pretty much a given these days, no matter what you're shopping for).

I would further recommend that if you're looking for deals, you might also consider used or refurbished gear. The biggest drawback to going this route, of course, can be that you may be purchasing an item that is no longer under warranty, so do keep that in mind. However, generally my shopping experiences on the used market have been very positive when it comes to buying pre-owned audio gear.

Amazon.com typically offers used options along with the items they sell, most of which are sold by third-party dealers. Other sites like eBay can offer good options on the used gear just as well; but if you're wary of buying used gear from retailers online, don't rule out pawnshops, which can be an excellent way to find great deals on used gear just as well, with the added benefit of being able to see the item in question before throwing your money down.

Something else that will often save you money in the long run, especially if you aren't into buying used equipment, is to purchase bundles instead, like the **PODCASTUDIO-USB Podcasting Bundle** by Behringer that we discussed earlier in this book. All-in-one kits like this will not only save you some money a lot of the time, but they will also provide you with everything you need to start podcasting from the ground up.

However, if I were going to recommend what I consider to be the ultimate podcasting bundle for anyone who is *really* planning to get serious about their craft, Cliff Ravenscraft's Podcast Equipment Package features the entire kit and kaboodle, including a Heil PR-40, a Mackie 1402-VLZ4 Mixer, Sony MDR-7506 headphones, and much more for a total of $1,599 (and he even includes shipping with that cost to U.S. customers). You can check out Cliff's different gear packages over at his website: http://podcastanswerman.com/equipment/

To summarize, the benefits of using gear like the devices we've covered in this section are primarily that the signal going into your recording setup will already be great sounding, thus limiting the need for much editing after the fact. Some podcasters may still wish to include additional processing after they've finished recording, either by using audio editing software, or as some might prefer, by using a service like Auphonic.com (or any combination of these). That said, for those interested in using audio software that might improve the quality of the shows you're producing, in the next section we'll look at a few more options that, while slightly more expensive, have become industry standards for their strength in creating professional digital audio.

Doing it "In the Box": Digital Audio Recording Software

Here, I want to feature a short section on audio editing software, since up until now we have primarily only discussed **Audacity**, a free (and very popular) audio editing program among podcasters (for more on that subject, see Chapter One). Programs like these aren't on the "hardware" end of things, but they certainly fall under the category of gear many serious podcasters or audio engineers (or both) may like to use. Generally, these programs will offer you greater flexibility, along with added features that will give you effects and capabilities on par with a lot of professional recording studios.

The first program you may want to consider is **Adobe Audition**, a professional audio editing utility that supports single and multi track interfaces. While many would argue that Audition has never caught up to Avid's **Pro Tools** for music production, Adobe's audio editing offering has become one of the industry standards in radio production, which as you might have guessed, was the same line of work where I first encountered it (in fact, in my early days of radio, there were still a few CPUs around our station that had the earlier Cool Edit program installed on them, which later became Adobe Audition). There are benefits, as well as drawbacks, to each program, a few of which we'll go over here.

For starters, in recent years we have begun to see the advent of "The Cloud", which is, to put things simply, an intangible area within the World Wide Web where creative things and stuff we want to save go and live when we aren't using them. Back in the old days, you could buy a program, which was sold to you on a CD-ROM disc, and from there you just inserted it into your computer, and installed the program… simple as that.

Yeah, that's not how they do things anymore.

These days, when you go to buy your programs, often you will purchase them almost exclusively online, where they are downloaded (or sometimes only accessed) entirely from the web. This has been both to create ease in accessibility, as well as to help the software industry find ways to curb pirating and illegal downloads, which ends up having its ups and downs for paying consumers.

Adobe's setup is still pretty interesting, if not admirably so. How it works is they offer you subscriptions to the Adobe Creative Cloud, which begin with allowing users access to photo editing tools (i.e. their basic Photoshop package) for as little as $9.99 a month. The next tier of pricing allows access to any other single program in the Adobe Suite, which includes Audition; access to a single program in this way is $19.99/month for an annual plan (otherwise, it's $29.00 for just one month at a time without the annual commitment. They also have a multitude of pricing options that include special rates for existing customers, individuals, businesses, students, and educational institutions). The more expensive plans they offer will allow you access to Adobe's entire catalogue of creative production software for a reasonable monthly fee.

The bottom line is that if you want to use Adobe Audition, you'll need to have a subscription to one of the Adobe Creative Cloud plans that includes the program. Although there are a number of benefits to this pricing model, one of the biggest drawbacks is that in order to use these Adobe products, customers now have to pay for them indefinitely; there is no such thing as a single, one-time purchase anymore (and let me tell ya, the response hasn't been entirely favorable on that front; just take a look at the "criticism" section on the Wikipedia entry for "Adobe Creative Cloud" for a concise overview of the kinds of flak they've gotten since instituting the changes). Customers also will essentially require Internet access at all times in order to access the program; although this isn't generally a problem in the modern world, one can imagine circumstances where this still might end up being a bit hindering.

Pro Tools, which we mentioned earlier, remains an industry standard for music production. It has never been quite as popular among podcasters, and up until late in 2010, this was the case in part because the program worked exclusively with the audio interfaces its creators at Digidesign (now Avid) had created for it. In November of that year, this practice was abandoned, and versions of Pro Tools that worked as a standalone program were made available.

Presently, the full version of Avid Pro Tools 11 can be purchased for $699... so think of it like this: if you *really* want to upgrade to a professional recording program, and you're dead set on having one of the two professional options I've outlined here, one will cost you a flat $699, while the other will take you three years, give or take, to rack up that kind of cost... *and then you'll keep on paying for it monthly after that.* Then again, with upgrades and add-ons taken into consideration, you'll probably end up paying indefinitely for Pro Tools just as well.

It is not my aim to word this in any way that will hope to dissuade you from going with one or the other of these in particular; in truth, I have worked with both programs in the past, and while I love using Pro Tools in a recording studio for musical projects, when it comes to podcasting and radio production, I would choose Adobe Audition instead, any day of the week, and twice on Sundays. It just so happens that my personal preference is also the option that might cost you the most in the long run, although the incremental payments are small, and comparable to many other paid-for podcasting services. I think it's actually very reasonable.

For all you penny pinchers out there, fear not, because there is one final option I'll offer for consideration here, especially for Mac users like yours truly, and that is **Garage Band**. I actually like Garage Band pretty well, and while earlier versions of it seemed to be designed with podcasting a bit more in mind, the newest version is still a highly functional, and reasonably intuitive audio editing program. In fact, some of its editing features, as well as the vast array of effects like compression, equalization, and other utilities, are actually quite impressive, and I would stack them against some of the best I've used in similar audio editing configurations in the past. While many people complain about the cost of Mac products, part of what you're paying for is the number of quality utilities that come installed with your computer's OS. Plus, having owned two of them, I have found that in my experience, these computers could probably survive dust storms, monsoons, and tornadoes, in addition to lasting for years longer than any PC I've owned.

There are a host of other recording programs available on the web these days, but I have chosen to highlight a few of the more costly options because of the features they offer for editing and post production, which includes effects like compression, EQ, reverb, and other creative elements which you may like to use. As always, what I recommend above all else is looking at different options before you land on a decision (including any options that I haven't discussed here), and see what other people are saying about them. There is a wealth of information available freely on the web, and if you really want to succeed as a podcaster, learning where to find helpful info (especially before making purchases) is going to benefit you greatly in the long run.

One more thing you'll need to be able to do, despite whatever program you are using, is to make sure that it recognizes your microphone and other recording devices. Doing this will vary with virtually every different audio program you'll use, but in a general sense, you should be able to do it by navigating to the "Preferences" or "Audio Settings" tab (or some similarly-named tab), and first making certain that the program you're using recognizes the device you wish to use; if it's a USB device, it will generally show up in a list along with other available devices, and can be configured simply by selecting it (fortunately, USB devices usually appear labeled as such when an editing program recognizes them). If you're using a device that plugs directly into a sound card or audio jack on your computer, it may appear under the name of the device itself, the audio input on the computer, or even more generally as the name of the company who manufactured it (sometimes this will also be labeled "built in input" or something more generic to that effect).

You may also need to designate the channels to which audio will be sent for playback while editing; these will generally be an audio input someplace on your computer, or it may be something the likes of one of the USB devices we've covered previously. In most cases, there is a "Help" tab that can offer further details, and don't forget that instructions on precisely how to configure your devices for recording and playback are usually available on the website of the company that created the software you are using. If all else fails, you can always try using a search engine to find out how others are doing it on the web. If you're having a problem, chances are good that someone else has had that problem too, and can help you with it.

Dialing In: Phone Hybrids and Skype for Making Calls

Since the 1940s, talk radio has existed as popular format that consists of a host who interacts with listeners and guests using a telephone line. George Roy Clough and Barry Gray were among the first jockeys in the United States who grew tired of just spinning records, and began incorporating live discussions and interviews into their shows. Gray had, in fact, employed this technique earlier on, by literally calling bandleader Woody Herman on the phone, and holding the receiver next to his microphone so that listeners could hear their conversation.

Fortunately, a lot has improved since then, thanks to the creation of what are called **telephone hybrids**, devices that split a phone signal and allow the connection of the phone lines with studio audio systems. Among the most popular models used by podcasters today is the **JK Audio Broadcast Host**, a digital phone hybrid that can be used to easily connect a land line telephone into your mixing board (there are a couple of similar models JK Audio offers as well, including their less expensive

Podcast Host, which runs for about $399, versus the $470 or so you'll spend on a Broadcast Host). I own a Broadcast Host, and have found this device useful at times for conducting telephone interviews where I need to call a guest on a landline phone.

Under optimal circumstances, a phone hybrid makes an incredible addition to any studio setup; however, many complain that despite carefully following the guidelines for setup and dialing in these devices, while one call will sound amazing, minutes later another call will be accompanied by noisy feedback, which creates audio that is nearly unusable. I have worked with more expensive phone hybrids in the past, including models by companies like Telos and Gentner, and generally when optimized for studios, these more expensive systems sound incredible. However, if you aren't in the market to spend thousands of dollars on a multi-line telephone hybrid system for taking live calls, I have to say that the money you would spend on a telephone hybrid (even a fairly decent one) might be used more wisely.

Here's how.

It's no secret that **Skype** has become the most popular call interface for podcasters. There are many reasons: for starters, since many podcasts aren't recorded while a live audience is listening, the potential for bad connections and audio drops aren't quite as worrisome, since they can be edited later. Also, Skype audio will usually sound better than a telephone, and with good equipment, it can often sound like the two parties were in the same room at the time of recording. To illustrate this, around the time I was writing this book, I was a guest on a nationally syndicated radio show called *Ground Zero with Clyde Lewis*, and using my podcasting setup and connecting via Skype, many listeners actually thought I was in the same studio with Clyde, despite being 2,640 miles away!

Finally, when it comes to taking telephone calls, Skype offers a **Skype Number** service, which allows you to make calls to, or receive calls from, a telephone. If you have a reliable Internet connection, and can minimize the amount of programs you have running on the computer you're using for Skype, nine times out of ten you will have nearly perfect audio for a Skype-to-phone call. Thus, in almost every instance, I have found this setup to be more reliable than using an inexpensive phone hybrid (and by "cheap", I mean one that will still cost you a few hundred dollars). What's even better is that since Skype is a free program, the minimal costs associated with obtaining a Skype Number and Skype Credit for making calls to phones far outweighs the kinds of problems associated with using hybrids.

Plus, there are a lot of cool tricks you can do by using Skype, especially if it's installed on more than one computer in your studio. Let's say you and your co-hosts are doing a podcast which you stream live to your website using a service like LiveStream or Google Hangouts for Air (which I'll explain in depth later). We'll also presume that each of you has Skype installed on your computers, and have Skype Numbers and Skype Credit available; all of this can easily be obtained for your Skype account at the company's website. You can use one account to call a guest, and then if you wish to take calls, you can use any secondary Skype accounts with associated Skype numbers to field calls from the audience; if your mixer has enough channels, you can simply run the audio output from each co-host's computer into a channel on the board, and an audio signal from the board back into each computer (so the callers can hear everything that comes through your board, and hence, so they'll hear you also. Just remember that this will work best by using a mix-minus configuration on your board, which reduces echo and feedback). In this way, you have effectively used Skype and a small group of computers to create a three-line calling system for live broadcast... and for pennies on the dollar.

But wait, there's more! A while back, I began to learn about some live shows that have taken this one step further by acquiring an inexpensive toll-free number to use for guest call-ins, which is then forwarded to the Skype number in question. I have tried this a few times, once I made the decision to take one of my podcasts to a live radio format with a network (my primary show, **The Gralien Report**, streams live every Monday night at 6 PM ET via www.KGRAradio.com). As you can see, there are numerous clever options you can use to integrate phone calls into your show, either for reaching guests, or to take calls from listeners, and with very minimal overhead costs.

Here's the Setup: Assembling Your Podcast Recording Studio

We've looked at a large amount of information over the last few sections, and along the way I've made some quality suggestions to you for different microphones, mixers, headphones, software, and other equipment you may want to use for creating the very best sounding podcasts. You may also find that there are particular pieces of equipment you'll come across and start to use that we haven't covered here, and that's fine too; there is always room to explore, experiment, and try new things with your podcasts. If there is one thing I can guarantee you, it's that no two podcasters will always do it the same way, or can really tell you there is just one way that "works" when it comes to podcasting.

Therefore, depending on the kind of equipment you'll choose, there can be just as much variety to the way you'll set up your studio. Here, we'll look at some basic configurations, and examine a few of my recommendations for the kind of setup scheme that has become ideal for a majority of podcasters.

In basic terms, here's what you'll be doing when you set up your studio:

➢ Microphones and other sources of audio (like a computer you may use for sound effects, Skype, etc) are sent into channels on the mixing board

➢ Audio processing can be added if desired, using a device like one of the compressors we discussed. This is often best achieved using a function on the mixing board called **channel inserts**, which allows effects to be added to a channel using a separate input that will both send *and* receive audio data via a single stereo cable

➢ Then the audio is sent from the mixer (usually from the output labeled "Main") and into a recording device, a computer equipped with audio recording and editing software, or both

That's the simple breakdown of what we'll be doing. Now we'll look more precisely at how to assemble a recording area with each of the primary pieces of equipment we've gone over up to this point, which will assume that you'll be using at least one microphone, a mixer, a set of headphones, and a computer equipped with editing and recording software like Audacity.

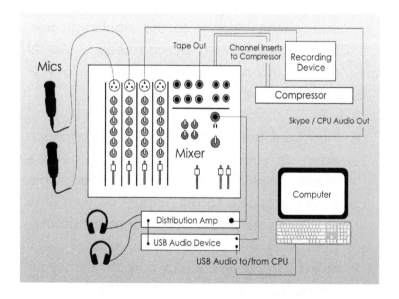

As we go over things, you may want to reference the diagram on the last page, which features a podcasting studio setup similar to what many professionals use. This is also similar to the setup I use, as well as studios that I've helped other podcasters build in the past.

➢ Connect your microphone to your mixer using an XLR cable. Most podcasters will use the first open channel on their board (furthest to the left) for this. If you have co-hosts, plug their microphones into the board using the next available input, keeping track of which microphone belongs to the inputs you use. It's a good idea to try and keep a mental note of this order, and to stay more or less consistent with this configuration

➢ Plug your headphones into the headphone insert on your board, or if you are using a mixing amplifier, run a ¼ inch stereo cable from this source to the "input" on your amp and plug your phones into one of its outputs

➢ Select one of the audio outputs from your board, such as the "Tape Out", and connect this to the audio input on your CPU (often this is labeled the "microphone" input). If you're using a headphone amp, it may be more convenient to use one of the channel outputs located here, rather than an output directly from the board, and feed a line from the amp into the CPU that way. This will send audio to a computer of your choosing, which can be used for capturing audio with recording software. Or, if you are capturing your audio with a standalone digital recording device, you can send audio from the Tape Out source into this device instead. As we've discussed before, it's far more reliable to do this, and pros like Cliff Ravenscraft and Ray Ortega swear by it.

➢ If you own a USB audio interface, such as **Tascam's US-2X2 USB Audio Interface**, you may try using this instead of plugging your equipment directly into a computer as described above (some mixers are equipped with USB functionality like this as well, which allows for direct, high quality connection to a computer). More than one of these USB devices can be used, which allows programs like Skype to be configured to one of the devices in the program's Audio/Video settings area, while a separate USB interface is dedicated to capturing audio from the board, and sending it to a source like Audacity or another editing program. You can achieve similar results with just one USB interface, but if funds allow, you may find that "two heads are better than one," as the old saying goes.

> Something many podcasters do when using Skype (and something I will recommend that you do just as well) is running what is called a "mix/minus" configuration, to reduce echo and feedback for your Skype calls. You'll want any audio that's sent to Skype (which allows your caller to hear your voice) to come from what are called **Aux Sends** on your board; most mixers will have these, even many of the less expensive models, though they are sometimes labeled "Mono Out" or "FX Send". Once a cable is connected from the Aux Send to the USB interface (or other audio input) on the computer running Skype, next you'll want to run an audio source on that computer into a channel on your board; this will allow you to control the Skype audio on that channel, just like a microphone or other audio source (you may also want to route this audio through a compressor or similar device using a Channel Insert, as we'll

describe in a moment). On this channel, you now want to make certain that the knob labeled **AUX**, corresponding with the output you used to send audio to Skype, is set all the way at zero. The reason for this is because this knob removes any audio coming from that channel in the mix that is sent to the Aux Sends; by doing this, you can ensure that the audio sent from your board into your Skype call *won't include the sound of the caller's voice*. This is important because removing their voice from the audio they hear coming from you will prevent them from having an annoying "echo" effect, which can be very distracting, and may even cause problems with the audio signal you're recording. With this in mind, you'll also want every other AUX knob on the channels with audio your caller will need to hear to be turned up to a decent level; otherwise, they won't hear these audio sources either. If you are using a phone hybrid to take phone calls, you will want to set this device up in the very same way.

➢ However, be sure *not* to use audio from the Aux Sends as the source audio you send to your recording unit; if you do, then your caller's voice will be removed here as well, which will be of no help to you! Just remember, Aux Sends go to Skype, and Tape Out goes to the recorder... easy as that!

➤ While we're on the subject of Skype audio, you'll also want to be sure to go into Skype's Audio Settings under the "Preferences" tab, and disable the "automatically adjust microphone settings" feature. This feature is designed to help regulate the volume level of the audio coming from your computer, which will often vary greatly in volume level if you are using a built-in laptop microphone. The result is that *all volume* coming from your computer, including background noise, will be automatically raised or lowered based on what Skype interprets as you not talking loudly enough, etc. Disabling this feature will ensure that your call volume remains consistent, and if you're using a professional recording setup like we're describing here, that's already been taken care of, hasn't it?

As described earlier in this section, using a device like Behringer's MDX-4600 Multicom Compressor/Limiter/Gate will help to greatly improve your sound, by allowing you to remove a lot of background noise and other low-level, but often annoying sounds like the room noise picked up by condenser mics, as well as hissing from a noisy Skype or phone connection. There are a couple of ways to achieve this, but the best involves using the **Channel Inserts** on the respective channels you wish to compress, and connect them to the compressor using a stereo cable (1/4 inch TRS or "Tip Ring Sleeve" Stereo on one end, to a dual 1/4 inch TS or "Tip Sleeve, Mono" cable. Note that the colors on the stereo cable are usually gray (or white) and red. Gray is the "send" side, while red is the "return" side). If this sounds like foreign language to you, podcaster Ryan Urlacher's great tutorial, "How to hook up and use Behringer MDX4600 Compressor Limiter Gate Podcast", can be found at this link: www.youtube.com/watch?v=A7UPaZYzTkY

This, in essence, completes the setup process. Keep in mind that you may be using more or less equipment than what I've described, or even the same general setup we have looked at here, but with different brands of equipment which each have slightly different functions from one to the other. As I've said already, there is no single "right" way to put together your setup, although I would argue that there certainly are a lot of *wrong* ways, which is why I've tried to outline a lot of those pitfalls for you along the way. Whatever setup you decide to use, keep in mind that you want to maintain a reliable recording setup that is not likely to result in audio being lost if, God forbid, your neighborhood experiences a power outage while you're doing your show. You'll also want to spend enough on quality equipment that will optimize the sounds going in, and of course, at least utilize some simple audio processing afterward (like Auphonic) to smooth things out before your finished audio is made available for download. I know I'm probably being redundant by now, but it really is a fairly simple process, despite the different methods employed by professional podcasters, and the formula for getting good results still remains a fairly consistent process. Trial and error helps too, so try different things that cater best to the setup you have, and the sounds you're trying to achieve.

Finally, if all else fails, you can always head to the Web and see what others are doing. There are a multitude of great articles and videos online that offer tutorials for setting up podcasting equipment, and throughout the writing of this book, I've even stopped several times to go online and look at how other podcasters may do things differently from me, in order to provide you with the most efficient, clear-cut ways of achieving great results; and rest assured, there are plenty of times where I've found myself saying, "why didn't I ever think of that!" As you've already seen, I've linked a few articles and tutorials like these along the way, and more will be featured in the appendix section in the back of this book.

Having your gear set up properly will be chief among the elements that will help your production quality become top notch. However, it also helps to know a bit about how to set up your mix, and when necessary, how adding and removing frequencies, edits, and audio processing can be used to improve the sound of the audio files you create. Therefore, now that our setup is complete, it's a good idea for us to look at a few things that anyone producing and mixing audio will want to keep in mind as they work.

Even if you have no experience with mixing and editing audio, there are a few things I've learned over the years that anyone can implement to help get a better sounding mix, and we'll look at some of those things right now.

A Few Notes About Mixing and Audio Editing

For one to attempt to offer just "a few notes" about a subject as broad as audio editing would be similar to saying you wish to write a short encyclopedia. There is so much that can be said about what it takes to *really* understand how editing and mixing works, and what someone can do to improve the sounds they create.

Still, I try to configure and work with my gear in a way that reduces the need for editing as much as possible once the recording is complete. Generally, since I produce many of my shows as live broadcasts, the only things I will edit out are things like commercial breaks that aren't included on the podcasts I post later, or any minor hiccups or glitches, which I note along the way as I'm recording so I'll remember to come back and check on them later (keeping a notepad handy while you're podcasting is great for noting areas you may want to come back and visit later like this, just in case there are problems with the audio that can be fixed with edits afterward).

Rather than to try and amass information for an authoritative text on how audio editing works, which would require having to explain *all* the functions of many different combinations of programs and gear, what I recommend instead is relying on manuals, websites, and documentation associated with the program(s) you may choose to employ. Sure, it may be universally true that nobody likes reading user manuals; but doing so can often save you a lot of trouble by arming you with important information that will help reduce problems that may occur later. Also keep in mind that when it comes to working with various gear, there are countless videos uploaded to sites like YouTube by users just like you and me, which will often do a brilliant job explaining anything you would like to know when it comes to technical specifics of a certain device or program you may be using.

However, there are some general principles about mixing audio that I will include here, which I feel will help you tremendously, aimed at helping limit the amount of editing you'll have to do later:

> As you're setting up your studio environment, before you begin podcasting it's always wise to spend a few sessions learning the way your equipment works, and dialing in volume and other settings accordingly. Be mindful of how everything sounds, including the sound of your own voice. I like to begin with all knobs set to 12 o'clock (this is usually what audio engineers refer to as a **flat EQ**, with "all

knobs at noon"), and then by listening carefully through headphones, speak into your microphone, and listen for whether there are frequencies like high end (treble) or low end (bass) that are overpowering. Another hint is to turn your headphones to a comfortable volume level, and then *add just a little more volume*, so that the mix you're hearing is ever so slightly louder than what you may be comfortable hearing (but not so loud that it's painful; we don't advocate hearing loss here). I have found that this will help give you a much clearer representation of what you're hearing, and will help you better discern between the overpowering frequencies as you're setting things up.

➤ The master volume control on your mixer (along with the other faders on your board) will have a marker indicating what is called "unity", which you can use as a sort of general guide for where you'll want your faders to be. I have often seen people riding their volume levels all the way up on *every* channel; you don't need to do this to obtain a good sound. In fact, it may actually cause your recordings to sound *worse* if your levels get so loud that clipping or distortion occurs.

➤ If you have separate gain controls along with the volume knobs or faders on your board's channels (as most do), another technique is to set your faders on each channel to "unity", and then adjust the gain control to even out the volume levels between your channels (since some microphones or other signals going in will be louder than others). Most boards will have an LED indicator showing where the volume levels going in will register; use this as a visual aid while dialing in your levels. If your board setup will be remaining more or less the same over time, setting up your board in this way will help you know exactly where your levels on each channel need to be more quickly in the future.

➤ One thing I definitely recommend is keeping your various volume levels below, or at very least equal to, your master volume. In the world of music production, as well as running sound in a live setting, keeping your input signals a few decibels below your master level is fundamental to obtaining a good sound, since this allows for what is called *headroom*. Simply put, headroom is space left in a mix in case there are any loud, sudden noises. If a noise is loud enough, it may overdrive the channel in question, resulting in *clipping*, as I noted a moment ago. Having headroom will help prevent that from ever happening, since you can always boost the volume of your completed show in a digital editor like Audacity during post-production.

➢ Having problems with clipping is especially going to be the case if, rather than using a mixing board, you're actually running your equalization entirely inside a computer (there are a few podcasters I know, especially those with a music background, who prefer doing things entirely with recording software, rather than a mixing board. Ten to one, I prefer a physical mixer for podcasting, because of the channel allotment and control it allows for a variety of situations). A quick web search will show you that, depending on the kind of digital recording equipment you're using, one can easily set their levels too high, causing certain channels to be loud enough to overdrive the internal summing bus; this is basically the orientation of the channels running though a mix. So pull back that volume a bit, buckaroo!

➢ Don't go crazy with your tone knobs either; I see a lot of people who think that by cranking the low end controls, they will magically cause themselves to sound more like Barry White when they talk into a microphone. I once observed a fellow broadcaster who, already blessed with a resounding bass presence to his voice, seemed to think that turning the bass controls on his mic channel *all the way up* would somehow help convey this over the microphone. That is entirely unnecessary, and in the long run, it may even cause problems with low-end frequencies in the final audio file you upload. I always begin by dialing in my levels at 12 o'clock, and then making adjustments from there. A simple rule here is to *take away before you add anything*; for instance, if you think your channel has too much high-end (treble), turn the high-end frequency knob back a bit, rather than adding to the low-end to try and compensate for it.

➤ Since we're talking about frequencies that may be standing out, once you've removed any offending High, Mid, or Low tonalities beginning with your primary microphone channel, you may also add (with moderation) to any areas on the frequency band that seem lacking (most people in radio and podcasts do like to add a bit of bass, and while I agree that this helps and sounds best with most microphones, as I've said, just try not to get carried away with it). Repeat this process for any channels with microphones your co-hosts may be using, and then as a final measure, try to balance the volume levels so that each microphone has a good, consistent volume in relation to the others. (Hint: use the LED volume indicator, which most mixers have, to help you determine visually whether any levels are exceeding others).

➤ Once you have dialed in the frequencies and gain levels on your microphones, try testing other audio sources, such as music, Skype, or sounds you bring in from a computer, and find out where they can comfortably sit so that they do not overpower the sound of your voice. As a general rule, keep music a few decibels *below* your microphone volume, and while Skype or phone can be a bit closer to your mic levels, it still might be wise to keep those channels a bit lower as well, since sources like phone audio tend to accentuate high and mid frequencies that can easily become overbearing if you aren't watching them. Remember, if necessary, you can dial in the tone on these channels as well, using the "remove first, then add" technique outlined above for setting up your microphone.

> When playing music beneath your voice, don't be afraid to work the fader control for that channel to bring the music levels down as you begin speaking. However, I always like to advise that the music volume shouldn't be too loud to begin with; keep it a bit lower, enough so that if you were to begin talking, your voice would already be clearly and easily heard over it. Then, very gradually, fade the music beneath your voice as you talk; you can use the same process in reverse by gradually bringing up the fader for the channel featuring music to create a soft bed of music behind your voice when, for instance, you're ending a show, or going to a

break, etc. As far as other ways you might employ sounds and music, just use your imagination, and consider ways you have heard sound effects used on other shows and podcasts. Your imagination is the limit, but as I've advised, it's good to make sure your microphone levels are noticeably (but not *too* obviously) louder in the mix.

With this general setup, you will have hopefully arranged your audio levels in a way that the sounds you produce are well mixed coming right out of the board, without any overpowering signals or frequencies. Additionally, if you've decided to use a compressor/limiter in this configuration, you'll find that the levels you've dialed in are smoothed out vey nicely, leveling the volume of all the microphones and generally improving the sounds you are creating. With a setup like this, you'll likely have very little editing to do afterward, and as a final touch, programs like Auphonic will smooth out the audio levels even more, helping to ensure you'll have a professional, even-sounding consistency to your recordings.

Of course, mistakes will still happen from time to time. There is just no getting around that 100% in every instance, and so there will be times where you may need to go back and make edits with your audio software. When doing this, a general key to remember, when editing the human voice, is to try and remove mistakes beginning and ending in silence, where the audio waveforms are flat-lined at "zero". Doing this will help keep your edits seamless, and when doing so, also be mindful of areas where you or your host have stopped to take a breath; nothing sounds more unnatural than to make a bad edit where an obvious cut was made in the middle of a breath. Your goal is to remove only what you have to, and to try and keep the audio sounding as natural as possible while doing so.

If something was badly botched enough during the primary recording session, you may also want to go back and "punch in", which essentially means you record a segment afterward that replaces the area where the problem had been beforehand. If you do this, be sure, once again, that you make your edits as carfully as possible, and that any audio you add or remove afterward is adjusted carefully enough that your finished edit sounds natural alongside the original portions of the recording.

Finally, within our discussion about mixing and editing audio, the program you are using may also allow you to add things like compression, limiting, and other effects to the final audio files you produce. I'll admit that while I generally don't make very many edits to the shows I've recorded, I'm still a big fan of doing a bit of final processing during the "post" phase, where I may add a layer of compression to tighten up the final sound of the audio before making a show available for download. But I'll warn you, once again, not to get *too* happy with compression and other audio effects. There are some podcasters I've heard over the years who seem to have little understanding for what actually sounds *good* on an audio recording, and it's easy to tell when the audio file you're listening to has been poorly edited, or even just processed *too much*. If you want people to enjoy listening to your shows, using a little compression to beef up your voice is a far cry from making yourself sound like a giant slab of meat talking through a rusty tin can. Natural, plus a little, is the key to sounding good.

Acoustics in the Element: Other Ideas & Considerations for Your Studio

Before we conclude our discussion of the podcasting studio, I wanted to take a moment to talk about the environment where you'll be recording, and specifically, the actual room you'll be using for your studio, which in many cases can be as important as any equipment you'll plan to use. Though you may not have given much thought to this up until now, everything about the environment, from the ceiling height and furniture arrangement in your studio, to the time of day that you'll be doing most of your recording, can affect the quality of your shows. Let's consider a few examples.

I can't count the number of times I've been on a show with another podcaster when, suddenly, an explosion of dogs barking interrupts us, following the materialization of a mailman nearby that caused every canine within a three mile radius to go nuts. Or maybe the podcaster in question has kids, and as they're arriving home from school, the amount of sound occurring in the background could be likened to a conflict between two small, but well-armed militias. Then, as the kids begin to log onto the Internet and look at Facebook or play videogames, the sudden drain on the bandwidth causes the connection to bottom out so badly that we'd get better results in our basements using 40-year-old HAM radios than trying to use Skype for calling.

The point here is simple: when you begin podcasting, you'll begin to see that you'll start finding a natural rhythm for things, which will include the time of day you'll begin setting aside for recording your shows. As you're doing this, take into consideration the kinds of things that may occur around your home or office during the day that could hinder your ability to produce a quality recording. In my experience, I've found that generally prior to noon, or sometime after 6 PM are best suited for podcasting in my case, as these times are less likely to include the ambient noises of lawnmowers, school buses, barking dogs, children playing, and phones buzzing or ringing off in another room.

For many, it just may not be as simple as being able to plan around the activities of the day to help ensure that every podcast will sound its very best; and to this, I can only say that an alternative may be to actually create a studio environment that reduces such external influences, using sound proofing and noise cancellation materials in a room dedicated solely to your podcasting operation.

Soundproofing is the process of improving the sound quality in an environment, using constructed material that is resistant to the passage of sound either through walls, or even within the environment itself. There are a number of materials that can be purchased online that will reduce things like echo and reverberations that occur from within a room, which may negatively affect the way your podcast sounds. Using a dynamic microphone and a noise gate amidst your effects processing will help some with this, but it also helps to have a room that efficiently uses soundproofing gear to further optimize your sound.

Popular materials that help with this are foam pads and hanging baffles that use what is called an *anechoic* design, which usually features wedge or pyramid-shaped patterns that prevent echo within a room. Foam padding like this can be bought online (I recommend you visit www.soundproofing.org for a comprehensive overview of anechoic materials, as well as options for purchase). There are even soundproofing paints available today, which help reduce the midrange sonic frequencies that the human voice falls within.

However, such materials are often rather costly, and therefore a lot of podcasters have opted to use more cost-effective alternatives. Many years ago, while helping a friend of mine move out of her previous home, we were having a hard time loading a rather large noise-cancellation wall onto the rental moving truck, which my friend's son had used in their basement while practicing guitar. She asked if I might want to use it for anything, to which I replied, "absolutely!" I still use this same sound wall in my studio today.

But when it came to the other three walls in the studio, I knew we'd need to use something to help reduce any reverberation, and so I purchased large 9' x 5' sections of carpet, which I secured to the existing bare walls in the room that became my studio. These carpets were each bought for less than $20, and have done a remarkable job at improving the sound quality for what little I spent on them, in addition to matching the sound and look of numerous professional studios I have visited over the years.

Another interesting idea that I've seen people try elsewhere is substituting the "eggshell" shaped foam mattress toppers, which often can be bought in bed-sized sheets (appropriately enough!) for roughly double the cost of the carpet pieces I described above. My pals Cam and Kyle from the

Expanded Perspectives podcast did this in their studio for a time, which they built as a separate room in Kyle's home, complete with its own air

conditioning! Not only is it a cool, cozy little studio, but also the sound deadening effect they were able to achieve was spot-on (though I should note, they have since upgraded to professional anechoic foam material).

Until now, I've been focusing almost exclusively on the devices and gear, software, and online services you will use as you begin your foray into the world of podcasting. We've covered a lot of effects, equipment, and tricks, as well as some of the "do's and don'ts" you'll want to keep in mind along the way. Finally, we've assembled the gear you've bought, and discussed the studio itself, and what factors about the studio environment will help make the difference between a quality show, and just anybody sitting in a room full of microphones.

Now, we're about to completely change gears, and once again look at an entirely different approach to how you can create a podcast. This third method will incorporate elements of doing things on the fly, as well as keeping things within a reasonable budget; but the central focus will be taking a podcast with you anywhere you go, and doing it with or without your ideal studio setup. I'm going to show you an insanely simple traveling setup I've used in the past, and we'll examine a few similar ways you can take your podcasts with you anywhere the road may lead, while still getting quality results.

What we're about to discuss, however, will teach you more than just how to take a podcast with you on the road. What follows will serve as the building blocks of a philosophy that, I feel, is the foundation of learning to liberate yourself from the mundane and the everyday, as well as harnessing the freedom to take what you love, and bring it with you anywhere you go. It is this ability to do what you love, without the burden or restriction of having to do it any one way, or in any one place, which I have found to be fundamental to knowing true freedom; or at least, as true as it can ever be known in the adult world of taxes, speed limits, and responsibility that we face in our modern lives.

The process I'm describing is the heart of what it means to be a Maverick Podcaster; while most people want to get their work done in the office and then get away from it, those who learn to create businesses that they can manage from anywhere they go are the ones who understand what true freedom is all about.

CHAPTER FOUR: ON THE ROAD

What would you be willing to do to be truly free? I think most of us have asked ourselves this question before. It is as old as we are, since the ultimate goal of living is, and always has been, to be able to do so freely, without restraint, and with optimal enjoyment of our time here on Earth.

A lot has changed since the days our ancestors spent roaming the land, gathering food and evading capture by larger, faster beasts than they were. Yes, they were "free" to do as they pleased, with no obligation to have to work jobs, pay bills and taxes, and conform within society like we do today. The concerns of early humans were few, in fact, aside from the daily struggle to survive, and to avoid dangers which modernity does help protect us from today. It was through our ancestors learning to survive in this way that modern humans came to possess the vast knowledge we now have of the universe, and with it, ultimate control of our surroundings. It didn't matter whether we were faster or stronger than our foes; the human mind succeeded where others could not, and in this case, "survival of the fittest" meant having the ability to think creatively in ways our enemies could not.

Creative thinking is at the heart of all modern technology, and through it, we've been afforded far more comfort than those before us ever had. With that comfort, there is also a degree of complacence; many of us simply don't realize all the tools at our disposal that allow us to make meaningful changes in our lives, and the lives of those around us. We've become stale and indifferent in a lot of ways.

Lets just be honest: the majority of us seem perfectly happy finding a small niche to exist within, whether that be an office, or a construction site, a garden, or a restaurant, and as long as we're getting by, we're fine with staying there... maybe forever.

Then there are others among us who go on to achieve greater success, perhaps through years of study in college, or maybe through learning by trial and error the right (and wrong) ways to succeed in a particular field. Some of these people have the drive it takes to launch their own businesses, and a smaller number of these are lucky enough to find success with it.

There is absolutely nothing wrong, by the way, with finding a place where we feel like we "fit" and staying there, whether that be a small position with a larger, national corporation, or being the top dog in a business that you own. As times have changed, perhaps our definition of what freedom is has changed as well, and fundamental to this new definition of freedom is learning to recognize what in life brings happiness to us, and to those we care for.

With that in mind, I think there is a better question many of us could be asking ourselves today, rather than "what would I be willing to do to be free?" That question is: *if you had the freedom to be doing anything you wanted, what would that be?*

Think about this for a moment. What would you be doing, right now, if there weren't a job to be at bright and early tomorrow, or mouths to feed nearby, or bills that had to be paid on time?

Let's not overlook the virtue in those everyday tasks like working a regular job, which inspired philosopher Adam Smith to consider the numerous social benefits, though perhaps often unintended, that result from our individual daily actions. The virtue of keeping food on the table and providing for our families is perhaps among the greatest virtues, as it is the essence of putting the needs of others above our own, which often can bring us individual joy just as well. Even bills, while frustrating for those of us who have to pay them (especially during leaner times) can fall under

Smith's vision of that "invisible hand" that moves society forward in unexpected and meaningful ways. We all have a small part to play, in other words, in the greater common goals of humanity.

Still, what if there were ways you could be pursuing the things you are most passionate about, and succeeding at using them as the vehicle for your prosperity? What if indulging your interests could still ensure comfort of hearth and home, and that obligations like bills would still be accounted for? Would the work it would take to get there be worthwhile, if the result were a new kind of freedom, different from what you may previously have known?

The World Wide Web has become a fertile proving ground for those seeking the "new freedom" we're speaking of here. Just to be clear, when I say "new freedom," I use this to describe removing yourself from being dependent on external entities to ensure your success (not some vague Orwellian reference, under which the only freedom we can know in the modern world is a "freedom" that exists amidst greater compromises with the state, for instance). You may also be asking yourself, what's so "new" about it? Aren't we just describing entrepreneurs, which have been around for as long as there have been concepts of how to provide a service to the public, and profit from it?

Well, yes and no. Yes, here we are describing entrepreneurship, but we are also describing a new breed of entrepreneur who has learned the long-sought art of working smarter, not harder. To be clear, I am one who also believes that there is simply no substitute for hard work; but hard work can be done in an intelligent way too, which minimizes time and effort put behind unnecessary or fruitless tasks.

Notice here that in the context of pursuing your passions and making them the focus of the work you do, I have avoided using the word "happiness" interchangeably with that of "freedom." There is a tremendous difference between shaping your lifestyle around independent endeavors that will help emancipate you from the need for building someone else's dreams in order to make a living, versus your general outlook on life and living. While each of these may contribute to the other, I believe that happiness is something you can choose, or at very least, that perhaps sadness is something you can choose to reject, within reason.

The "new freedom," while perhaps not innate, is something that can be achieved to varying degrees through persistence and hard work. And yes, having a positive outlook on things can certainly help determine how successful you will be at this. In fact, it may be integral to your ultimate success, or failure.

How I Went On A Road Trip While Launching a Side-Business That Helped Fund It

When I first made the commitment to start podcasting on a weekly schedule, it was both liberating and terrifying all at once. Each and every week, I had a new show to look forward to doing, and in equal turn, I knew that the success of my podcasting would forever have to rely on whether I chose to stick to this schedule or not. When the latter thought ever crossed my mind, I would sometimes shudder, knowing that it was going to have to be either all, or nothing. In other words, if I wanted to succeed, I would have to be in this for the long haul.

Looking back, I realize now that I had been thinking about this all wrong. There was nothing restricting about what I was doing by getting deeply into podcasting; in retrospect, it was actually one of many significant steps I've taken toward liberating myself from the kinds of restrictions I had previously, and as a result, it has also helped me become more successful.

For the first three years or so, I did very little in the way of trying to monetize my shows. I did install a PayPal button on my site, which allowed any kind souls who stopped by to drop me a donation of five bucks here and there, which might cover a little of my web hosting expense, or maybe allow me to buy another coffee, which I probably needed about as badly as a shape-shifting were-jaguar needs bullet-shaped shards of silver propelled into its ribcage.

For some time, I had begun to consider hosting a subscriber area for one of my podcasts, The Gralien Report, which would offer exclusive content for people at a reasonable monthly fee. I put this off for what must have been months, which then became years, while I watched other podcasters making money (if not making a living) doing their shows, and building online enterprises around these programs with websites, social media, and other elements that helped them expand their reach.

In the early months of 2014, I had been working remotely as an editor for a small magazine that had been operating for several decades in Minneapolis. The editor contacted me, wondering if I might be willing to come up for a few days and work with their staff on some technical issues they were trying to resolve. I knew I had some travel that would be occurring later that month, so as I made my plans, I figured I would first stop for a few days in New York, where I planned to catch up with my fellow podcaster Christopher McCollum, his girlfriend, and their King Charles Spaniel, Daisy, for a few days. Then it would be on to Minneapolis for a week, and Greenville, South Carolina after that for a brief stop between trips to Savannah, Georgia (where a friend at the nearby naval base helped me obtain clearance to tour a nuclear submarine... long story for another time). After this, it was further south to Amelia Island, Florida for a performance with my band, where I would catch an early flight out of JAX to Fort Smith, Arkansas, to attend a conference in Eureka Springs the next morning. The entire trip would have me on the road for about 29 days, one night of which I spent back at home in Asheville, North Carolina.

All the plans were set, and everything looked like it was set to go off without a hitch. Then, life began to happen: a sudden series of expenses that included new tires for my car and a host of other things all rained down on me at once, and with each day, my travel plans were looking more and more risky in terms of the expenses involved. Since I'd already booked flights to New York, Minneapolis, and Greenville, there wasn't going to be any easy way to cancel the trip, but if I followed through, funds were going to be tight, to say the least.

It always seems to be in moments of desperation like this that the best ideas happen. Some people would have freaked out and cancelled everything; others would have gone into debt with credit cards or personal loans.

In my case, I found myself thinking, "What better time could there possibly be to go ahead and launch that subscriber area for the website?"

I knew that this plan would certainly solve the problem of being able to recoup my expenses in the weeks leading up to and during the trip, but in equal turn, I knew that I would have to be working as I traveled, which brought into question the equally troubling issue of how I would be able to do my podcasts reliably, and without sacrificing quality using only a small amount of equipment I could carry along.

After doing some research, I put together a game plan, of sorts. I decided to build a separate area within my primary site, where I implemented a paid subscription plugin called **Wishlist Member** that, I must say, has simply worked wonders since I purchased it. The plugin creates an interface through which anyone can transform a Wordpress installation into a site that separates free and paid content with relative ease, and all at the administrator's choosing.

Having completed that, the general setup for the subscriber area was finished; I chose to use PayPal as the interface, and set up a proper business account for this, completing the backend of the subscriber content area and the payment system that would serve as its backbone. All seemed to be in perfect order, aside from that little issue of how I would do the podcasts without dragging an ungodly amount of equipment along with me on my journeys all over hell and, literally, half of Georgia. My accomplice in New York (being one of the cohosts on my podcast at the time) had a modest setup I would be able to utilize while visiting the Big Apple, but thereafter I would be left to my own devices.

It was time to build something new, and out of necessity, came invention... or at least something fairly close to it. It was under these circumstances that I stumbled onto what I have since begun calling **The All-in-One Anywhere Podcasting trick**, and right now I'm going to tell you how I did it.

In addition to that, we'll also look at a variety of other ways podcasting while traveling can be done, and how others have combined stripped-down versions of what they do at home to create portable systems for themselves, so that podcasting while traveling becomes painless, inexpensive, and even enjoyable.

How I Obtained Live Studio Quality on the Road with $174.99 and a Laptop

In the days leading up to departure, we launched what I dubbed **Gralien X** as my subscriber area; I'll never forget the hush that fell over the chat room of live listeners as my cohosts and I were doing our show the night of the announcement (that silence, funny enough, is often the surest sign that your audience is listening; remember that). As the subscriptions began rolling in shortly afterward, I had been considering the best ways to assemble a minimalist package that would achieve quality results for this while traveling, but still on a reasonable budget.

While flipping through a copy of *Podcasting for Dummies* by authors Tee Morris, Chuck Tomasi and Evo Terra, I came across mention of a small, portable microphone called the **Zoom H2n Digital Multitrack Recorder**, which is essentially a small condenser microphone with multiple microphone settings and channel recording capability, built into a device which records high quality digital audio all within a single unit. Today, there are several more advanced and updated versions of this microphone that have appeared, but I have found that for its modest cost, this particular model has a number of features that make it ideal for podcasting remotely, if your objective is to limit how much equipment you carry with you.

I was able to purchase this microphone in a small bundle that included an accessory pack with an SD Card, a cheap set of ear buds (I'll admit, these were useless), an 1/8-Inch-to-RCA Cable, and a 3.5mm Stereo Cable, as well as a small stand, a USB power supply, and a carrying case with a belt fitting attached. The entire bundle cost me only $174.99 (though I should note, I see that the cost of similar bundles have gone up slightly since the time of my purchase in 2014).

What's unique about this microphone is that in addition to having built-in recording functionality, the microphone also has features like mic patterns for omni-directional, polar pattern or "figure eight", and close pattern settings, as featured on many studio condenser microphones. The microphone also features digital compression settings that can be added, effectively achieving a decent-sounding processed signal right off the unit; combining a close-pattern "mono" setting with the compressor feature allowed me to nearly duplicate the in-studio sounds I achieved at home with a quality broadcast microphone. Finally, a stereo input for sending audio from an external source is also included, which can be controlled using a volume knob on a device like your laptop. For instance, lets say you decide to use iTunes to create a playlist you'll use to fire audio during your show; all you have to do is run a stereo 1/8 cable from your laptop's headphone jack into this input on the microphone, and while monitoring through headphones, you can use the computer's volume (or the fader on the iTunes window itself) to adjust the incoming audio levels in relation to the level of your voice as you speak into the microphone. With a little practice, the process becomes seamless, and within an hour of having received the microphone in the mail, I had configured it to function as an all-in-one portable podcasting setup with my laptop.

I had hoped that maybe this would sound decent, at least, but to my great surprise, there were times where I could compare the audio I recorded during tests with this minimalist setup to my normal studio sound, and the similarities were incredible. For the small investment, this setup was more than merely functional, producing great sounding audio that, apart from my laptop, would fit in a space about 1/3 the size of a shoebox. This setup worked fine with Skype as well; so as long as I had a reliable Internet connection, doing a live show remotely, or bringing on a guest during a recording, became equally feasible. Hence, as I traveled over the course of the next month, my podcasting didn't have to suffer as I made my way from one location to the next, recording audio sound bytes wherever I went to be used in future podcasts I produced.

The Tao of the Traveling Podcaster: Zen and the Art of Portable Podcasting

The portable podcasting setup I've described here is by no means the only way to achieve great results with podcasting while traveling, and depending on things like your budget, how light you like to travel as far as carry-on luggage goes, and a host of other things, there may be even better options for you.

For instance, my friends Graham and Darren of the Grimerica Podcast have carried only minimal equipment with them to events they attend, like microphones and computers. Then, upon arrival at their destination, they simply rent equipment from an audio facility in town to fill out their setup. That way, they can have full studio capability, without having to bring an entire studio along with them wherever they go. On the other hand, my friend Jim Harold, host of "TV You Grew Up With" and "The Paranormal Podcast" has recommended to me the **Audio-Technica AT2005USB Cardioid Dynamic Microphone**, which as I described earlier in the book, has USB and XLR functionality. This mic, paired with a device like an iPad, has helped Jim achieve quick, but reliable on-the-go recording in a variety of situations, such as walking the floor at conferences and conventions, and conducting brief interviews with guests and attendees while there.

By the way, if you're an iPad owner, there is one incredibly neat app that you should be aware of if podcasting on the go is going to be your thing. This is called **bossjock studio**, and for just $9.99, it's one of the most formidable podcasting apps I've come across. However, you don't *have* to own an iPad to access this program; bossjock works with your iPhone just as well, and considering the larger screens we began to see with the new iPhone 6 models, the functionality of an app like this is now more accessible than ever, and still able to fit in your pocket.

To look at just a few of the features bossjock offers, with it you'll be able to:

> ➢ Record your podcast and fire live intros, sound effects, and background music all from your iOS device

> ➢ Add compression, limiting, and other effects

> ➢ Create podcast-ready audio without any need for post production

- ➤ Access to iTunes, Dropbox, Soundcloud, Wifi, FTP, iTunes Share, AudioCopy, or even plain old-fashioned email

- ➤ Encoding functionality in a variety of formats

- ➤ Compatibility with a variety of external microphones like the Apogee Mic, IK Multimedia iRig Mic Cast, and Blue Mikey

There are a lot of other features you'll want to check out with this app, so look for bossjock (yes, it's all lower-case like that) in the iTunes store, or just visit http://bossjockstudio.com/ and you can read more about this incredible little app.

In fact, while bossjock is great for podcasting on the road with as little as an iPhone and a specially fitted microphone device like the **Apogee MiC**, I do know a few podcasters who use it in their studios just as well, much like radio producers have used digital sound playback devices for years while doing their live shifts. bossjock is a great resource for adding audio elements to your program while you're doing things live, just as well as being what may be, arguably, one of the best new tools for taking podcasting with you on the go.

Also consider the way a program like bossjock might work with another device we've talked about, like the Zoom H2n. Using the headphones output on your iPhone to send the audio to a microphone like this, you could use bossjock for your intro, sound effects, music, and other audio, while recording directly into the Zoom microphone. As you can see, this podcasting setup is in essence just an iPhone and a microphone!

Obviously, there are a number of options available to podcasters who are interested in taking what they do with them anywhere they go. Here again, in addition to teaching you about tools and techniques that will help you to become a pro at podcasting, I also want to emphasize the kinds of options available to you, especially when you begin to apply a bit of creativity to situations where you may have a certain need, but maybe not a clear idea of how you'll achieve it.

I should also note here that the "All-in-One Anywhere Podcasting Trick" we've discussed in this chapter is NOT a replacement for having a really good studio setup at your disposal. Ideally, a really serious podcaster will want to have gear for each setup, as the situation requires. That said, the gear we've looked at here does present a reliable way to create quality podcasts anywhere you go without having to lug around a ton of equipment. The more we begin to look at podcasting as something that can change your outlook on things, and in many cases even jump-start lifestyle changes that will help you free up more time, the more important I think it becomes to consider ways this hobby is something you can take with you anywhere.

And hopefully, learning to podcast actually will present life-changing opportunities for you. While this may not be the case for everyone, there is no way I can deny the profound effect it has had on my own outlook on things, from my way of thinking, to the way I look at things like business, self employment, and the broader relationship between humankind, technology, and the ways we process and share information.

The next phase of this book is going to look at things like how to find compelling content for your podcast; we'll also look at the differences between adding elements like music afterward, versus using sound playback to fire audio while doing it live. Speaking of "doing it live," we'll also spend a little time looking at how doing a live, streaming Internet radio show differs from a download-only podcast, as well as how the two can peacefully coexist, and the variety of ways you can incorporate things like live streaming and video into your podcast without spending an arm and a leg.

Finally, since we've talked a lot about how much you may or may not spend, it's only fair that we look at the various ways you can generate profit from doing your podcasts as well, and what kinds of programs and services will allow for it.

In essence, what we've covered so far puts all the tools in place for you; now it's time to examine what can effectively be called "Podcasting Theory," and how to use information and other tools at your disposal to help create the kind of podcasting experience that truly defines who you are, and how you will be perceived by your listeners.

CHAPTER FIVE: PODCASTING THEORY

The late Robert Hughes, acclaimed writer and critic of the arts, once said that, "a determined soul will do more with a rusty monkey wrench than a loafer will accomplish with all the tools in a machine shop." In the same spirit of determination, so may it be said of podcasting that no amount of fine equipment at your disposal will help you achieve what determination alone may bring you. This, and a healthy smattering of creativity applied toward the endeavor, will take you far.

Still, some fundamental knowledge will be required, which has been the purpose of this book. Therefore, with the discussion of tools largely behind us, in this section we will begin to look at taking what we have, and unraveling the *how* behind the *what*, in an attempt to break down the fundamental theory of how a good podcast can be made. This chapter will also focus on additional tools and services that can be used to assist in furthering one's success with the endeavor.

By now, you have probably listened to a number of podcasts yourself. If you haven't, then I strongly recommend that you put this book down right away, and don't come back to it until you've listened to several examples of what different podcasts sound like, what subjects other hosts address, what kinds of guests are featured in the interviews about subjects you find interesting, and what about these shows make them interesting and appealing to the ear.

Obviously, as expressed above, I think it's very important to listen to what other podcasts are doing. However, I also think it's time to draw the line as soon as one begins approaching the pure emulation of what other shows are doing, rather than creating original-sounding content of their own. While imitation is perhaps the sincerest form of flattery, it will also be obvious to active podcast listeners if you model your program and its sound too closely to another show you've listened to. There's nothing wrong with picking up ideas here and there, and finding clever new ways of borrowing elements that you can incorporate into what you do in a unique way. Just don't steal all your ideas from what other podcasters are doing.

Which brings us to even greater questions like, "if emulation is bad, then where *does* one go to look for good, original ideas when it comes to what can be done on a podcast?" Similar issues might involve whether or not audio like popular music can be played on your show (generally this is advised against, for legal reasons), as well as how to find reliable news and stories for discussion. And what about guests? Are there good ones to pursue, and bad ones to avoid, as well as good or bad subjects in general that a podcaster should be aware of?

It's time we look at all of these questions, and more, under the broader umbrella of "podcasting theory". It's the final proving ground that will determine the difference between mice and men, or in this case, the difference between the true podcaster, and the hopeless Howdy Doody with a hand up his hiney, being worked like a puppet by someone else's standards, while failing to credibly reproduce the excellence of those around them who are actually succeeding.

What follows will be a rapid-fire roundup of "final considerations," in addition to all the technical stuff we've already gotten out of the way... so lean in, and hang on.

What You Should Know: A Brief Look at the Legalities of Podcasting

As with any kind of media, there are a few legal considerations you may want to consider when it comes to podcasting. Chief among these are whether music, sound bytes, and other audio are legal for you to use, with similar considerations for written content produced by another party.

As a general rule, I advise podcasters to avoid borrowing from any kind of content, especially audio, for which they don't have permission to use. This includes popular music, since royalty payments and other industry considerations are generally not favorable when it comes to obtaining permission to use such material, both in terms of costs, and the general hurdles associated with the licensing process. There are some cases where I've known podcasters who actually did go to the trouble to contact artists about using their songs; but even after obtaining permission to use them, this still won't always protect you from getting into bothersome situations where you may have to provide things like written proof that the permission was indeed obtained.

One excellent example of this is when such content is featured on YouTube. In the past, I have had numerous talented artists send me recordings they've done, with full permission for me to use these songs on my podcasts (and in truth, when I've done so, they are often thrilled to hear their material featured on the show). Later, once I've uploaded these episodes to my YouTube channel, I will often find that any music that has been registered with entities like BMI will be flagged for third party content by Google's algorithms. Sometimes this merely results in a warning, but in more extreme cases, the entire audio track of the show you've uploaded may be removed, in addition to things like the video being unable to feature Google advertisements. Enough marks against you account could even result in your account being disabled, though this is generally uncommon.

Of course, YouTube does allow you to go through a process where you can dispute any such claims against your video, and provide written proof of your right to use the content you've featured. However, doing this on a case-for-case basis on every video you upload can become time consuming indeed. So what I've done in order to prevent having this problem, while effective, does require being musically inclined, or at least having friends who are. That's right, on my shows, I generally only feature music created "in house", specifically designed by me, or by someone I know, for use exclusively on my programs.

Naturally, you may be wondering, what should you do if you aren't a musician, or if you don't have gobs of friends out there that are just dying to make albums worth of material solely for use with your podcast?

First, I'd suggest you head on over to YouTube, and do a quick search for something along the lines of "royalty free music". Here, you can often find countless examples of music that is free to use in podcasts, videos, and other mediums. The creators may request that you give them credit for their work; others may require a small, one-time fee for licensing privileges. Still, this will get you access to music you can safely use on your shows. Just always be sure to read the descriptions on the content you find, and make sure that it is indeed truly "royalty free," or that any requests by the content creators are met before being used.

Keep in mind that the same considerations for the use of music may also apply to things like articles and blog posts just as well. In many cases, however, it could be argued that what you've featured on your show constitutes **Fair Use**, if it's only a snippet or short sample, and the content borrowed is relevant to a discussion or analysis. The truth is that, every single day, and all over the world, radio hosts and podcasters read news articles on their shows, and with little or no trouble, even in cases when something may not have been properly sourced. This is the nature of New Media, to an extent, but I still say that if you're going to feature a portion of an article or other written work on your program, try to keep it short as a general rule, and be sure to give credit to the source. If, however, the source in question has a disclaimer stating, "No part of this may be reproduced," I would steer clear of using this content completely.

Admittedly, the realm of Fair Use is a rather nebulous one. Article after article has been written about this subject, trying to illustrate the safe, legitimate areas where a content producer will remain "in the green," so to speak, when using third party content in various mediums. If you're ever in doubt, the fine folks at the Creative Commons Corporation feature a Podcasting Legal Guide at their website, a resource that may be able to help you beyond anything we've covered here thus far: https://wiki.creativecommons.org/wiki/Podcasting_L egal_Guide

I would even say that this is an invaluable resource, and although you (hopefully) may never encounter any problems with what constitutes Fair Use, etc, it would be wise to bookmark the link above and keep it in mind for future reference anyhow.

Going Live: Prerecording vs. the Live Broadcast

As we discussed a bit earlier in this book, talk programming of all kinds has its roots in live radio.

Of course, with the advent of podcasting, more and more people are able to join the revolution and have their voices heard, without having to have a broadcasting license with the FCC, nor a station with enough power to carry your voice along to radio receivers in homes and cars around the country. With a minimal investment, podcasts can be created easily within the comfort of your own home, and uploaded to the web for anyone to download at any time of their choosing thereafter.

So why, then, would we want to talk about doing a live broadcast of a podcast? Here's why: because just like traditional live radio, a podcast can be recorded "live", which gives the producers the benefit of things like interactions with a live audience through phone calls, chat rooms, and a number of other mediums.

Granted, doing a live show like this may not be for everyone. Some podcasters may feel like the requirements of live broadcasting, like having to get things "right the first time" is simply too stressful, which is indeed a benefit of being a podcaster in the first place: if you aren't happy with how something sounded while you were rolling tape, nothing is stopping you from going back and trying a second take (or even a third, fourth, fifth, and so on, if necessary). But if you are comfortable enough with your format and your live production skills (or better yet, if you have someone nearby to assist as a producer, and help you with cuing music, working faders, and other things a live radio show does), you may find that the energy of doing a live show is actually preferable.

If you decide to do a live show, there are a few things you'll want to keep in mind:

> Since things have to sound good at all times when streaming to a live listenership, make sure you've practiced balancing out audio levels as described in the section in Chapter Three titled, "A Few Notes on Mixing and Audio Editing." This will help you get an ideal balance before going to air.

> It's also wise to consider how your show will be formatted, and when (or if) you will incorporate things like commercial breaks, music, interviews, and other elements. Plan roughly how much time you'll want to spend on each element, and time it out within the general length you set aside for your show.

> If you plan to bring in guests via Skype or phone on your live show, this will be something you will need to plan for in advance. I recommend having your guest on

the line *before* you go live, or if using a service like Skype, plan to have their profile available in the Skype window so they can be called and brought onto the program in just a few short keystrokes.

> With guests, it is also wise to make contact before the live program, and let them know what to expect when they are brought onto the show. There is nothing worse than having a guest lined up, and then calling them only to get a busy signal, or if they *do* pick up as planned, their first question is something like, "uh, are we live?" As a courtesy to them, and to ensure the flow of your live program, make sure they know ahead of time what to expect during the interview.

With all these things in mind, it's also important that if you are going to go live, you first learn how it can be done. If your aspirations are to go beyond doing a single podcast, and launching a full-scale online radio network, services like Live365 can help you with every step of the way, in addition to offering affordable hosting solutions for live streaming. However, since this book is about podcasting, rather than live Internet radio, in the section to follow we will focus on free services that can be used to stream your shows to a moderately sized audience; alternatively, if you like the idea of doing your show live, and want a more "hands free" approach, you might consider searching online for small Internet-based talk radio networks, many of which are happy to add live shows to their rosters (though some may require hosting or production fees, based on their business model, traffic they receive, the number of shows they feature, and other factors).

The Maverick's Guide to Broadcasting Live on a Budget

If you've decided you really want to go ahead and take a crack at doing your show live, first let's try and alleviate some of the pressure you may expect to feel about your first time behind the mic with a live audience tuning in.

One of the greatest misconceptions about doing a live show is that, suddenly, you have hundreds, or even thousands of people that will be listening to you, scrutinizing your every word and ready to engage in the online equivalent of launching rotten tomatoes at you. To this, I say:

> Try to relax. Unless you're already famous, rich, or both, don't expect a mob of listeners

to arrive in swarms for your inaugural broadcast... which means that doing a live podcast like this will be a fun, casual opportunity to engage a modest portion of your audience in real-time.

➤ If, however, you have a tremendous following on social media, you might not really have to be rich or famous to generate enough interest in what you're promoting to have a good turnout for your first live broadcast. While this is indeed possible, if I were you, I'd still expect listeners by the tens, at most... not by the thousands. Audiences like this are grown over time, and while attainable, are harder to keep than most would imagine.

In fairness, of course there are some hosts out there who manage to get people to come out in droves for their live shows. You may even get to a point yourself where you become one of those online radio prodigies. Despite this, I have found that in recent years more people seem to prefer being able to listen on demand, rather than having to be in a specific place, at a specific time, just to be able to tune in to a show. Above all, I just wish for any budding podcaster to be realistic about this, and in equal measure, to understand how public preference is moving toward the ability to have shows that can be downloaded and listened to at any time; this fundamental truth is at the heart of what podcasting is, what makes it different from radio in the first place, and why the popularity of podcasting is so often referred to as being "revolutionary." But there are still benefits to doing a live show too, which is one reason I recommend combining the elements of both categories. With that in mind, we'll look at a few mediums here that can help you do this.

Ustream is among the most popular video streaming sites today. In fact, they bill themselves, according to their website, as "The leading HD streaming video platform." Notice that in that description they specifically state that they are a "video platform". This is a common thread between virtually all inexpensive live streaming options: they are designed for streaming HD video, and while they can be used with greater emphasis on the audio for things like podcasting, generally there will have to be some visual component included as well. The web address for their site is Ustream.tv.

LiveStream, with its similar sounding name, is a video streaming site that is also similar in function to the aforementioned service. Each of these services features a basic free plan supported by revenue from advertisements, which may interrupt portions of your broadcast. To avoid this, paid subscriptions that are ad-free are also offered.

Google Hangouts is one of the most interesting and formidable of the free live streaming options. Having used all three of the aforementioned services, this is the one I like the best, and have used the most, for a number of reasons that I'll explain in a moment. The way it works is a bit different from Ustream or Livestream, where you would log in to your account and use their control panel to orient your microphone, camera, and other elements for your broadcast prior to air. Since Google and YouTube are jointly owned, a Google Hangout is activated first by going to the profile page for your Google Plus account, and in the upper left hand corner, hovering over the dropdown, and navigating to the "Hangouts" tab that appears below it. In the new page that appears, you can scroll down and navigate to the area labeled "Hangouts on Air," and click the green button that says, "Start a Hangout on Air." This will allow you to name the Hangout, and set a time for it to begin. A box featuring the newly created Hangout will then appear in a new window, and to enter it, click the blue button labeled "Start", which has a camera next to these words. A new window will open with the Hangout screen embedded within, which features a number of apps you can use to control various functions of the live broadcast.

Here is where I found the Hangouts feature to be particularly useful. First, move your cursor over the Hangouts window (if it automatically identified the camera on your computer already, you may be seeing yourself in this window). Here, you will see a list of apps appear on the left side of the screen, as well as near the top. Navigate to the list of icons that appears at the top of the window, and select the gear-shaped icon labeled "Settings". In the window that appears; here you can select the camera, microphone source, and other settings you may wish to use. Select the proper camera, and make sure the audio source is the same that will recognize the audio coming from your mixer into your computer (in most cases, this will be the USB audio CODEC, but some may be using the computer's analog mic input to bring audio to their computer, so be sure to select the correct option). The fourth option here features a dropdown that defaults to the word "Voice". However, by clicking this, you can change the setting to "Studio", which will help optimize the audio settings for a live show featuring music and other sounds. Once you have changed all these settings, click the blue "Save" button at the bottom of the window.

Now hover over the app icons on the left side of the window, and locate the one called "Hangout Toolbox." Selecting this will cause a new tab to appear on the right side of the window, with a number of additional tabs and features. If you select the tab featuring the shape of a person's head and shoulders (on the far left near the top of this new tab), a panel will appear that displays features for what is called "Lower Third", which has options for entering text that will appear by your name at the bottom of the page, as well as a custom logo you can create yourself and upload. The next box down is labeled "Custom Overlay", and here, if you decide you *don't* want to stream video of yourself talking the entire length of your podcast, you can upload a larger, full-screen image that features something like your logo or podcast artwork, which will then appear in the Google Hangouts window instead. Doing this will effectively bypass the video option altogether, allowing you to proceed with doing your live show in your underwear, like any *real* professional would do.

Finally, in the lower right hand portion of the video window itself, you'll see an icon labeled "Links". Clicking this will open a window that gives you three options: the Event Page, the YouTube Page, and the Video Embed. Now let's say you wanted to stream this show directly to a page on your Wordpress site. All you would have to do is copy the text for the code in the third box next to "Video Embed", and paste this into the body of a post or page on your site. Doing so will embed an actual YouTube player on the page in question, which your listeners can then go to and play by visiting the same page on your site. Altogether, this is one of the simplest ways to create a customized live stream of your broadcast, and embed it on your own site.

As far as any drawbacks with this service, I have found that the Google Hangouts can tend to utilize a lot of resources. If you have a lot going on in other tabs and windows while running a Hangout, they may be prone to crashing, or other glitches that can occur from time to time. For the most part, the service is extremely useful, and considering all the features it offers at absolutely no cost, I consider it one of the most beneficial streaming options available to podcasters right now. Plus, your show is automatically uploaded to your YouTube account after you finish, which makes it available for your subscribers automatically. This is helpful because I have found that you will likely build a separate audience altogether with your YouTube subscribers, apart from those who get your shows with podcast programs like iTunes. As Smartphones continue to be optimized for streaming video content, more and more content uploaded to sites like YouTube will be accessed by users from their phones, so be sure not to miss out on having at least some of your shows available here.

There are other streaming options worth considering, such as using IceCast, Shoutcast or Live 365 to carry your own independent stream. Live broadcasting software like **Sam Broadcaster** also will function with a streaming service like Live 365, or one they can provide to their customers for a small fee, but unless you really want to prioritize a live Internet radio station over creating your podcasts, my advice is to stick with simpler, free services like Google Hangouts, which take a lot of the hassle out of things.

Turning Your Podcast into a Videocast

Having spent so much time here discussing video streaming services that can be used to broadcast your live podcast like a radio show, it's only natural that we would spend a little time looking at the differences between an audio podcast, and a video show, which we might effectively call a "videocast" for general purposes.

If done properly, adding the visual dimension to your shows can help to bring some of the thrill of a television talk show to your podcast. However, once again I'll advise that we be realistic about this: most of us don't have expensive live production equipment on par with the **NewTek TriCaster** models, which allow you to seamlessly mix cameras, video, titles, graphics, and other elements of a live television program into your shows. Fortunately for most of us, you also don't need to have one of these just to create a decent-looking videocast.

In fact, there are a number of ways that you can incorporate some degree of live video switching into your shows. For starters, if you have decided to hang with Google, another feature of their hangouts is that if you add other callers or guests to the broadcast, Google's streaming player will automatically switch to that person's video stream as soon as it detects audio from their source. While automated, this is still fairly limited technology, and can tend to be a bit buggy, although it gets the job done.

Another option for those on a budget is **WireCast**, a versatile video-streaming program that enables simple video edits along with quality audio, titles, graphics, and more, all for just a few hundred dollars. And here's a hint: a simple, free version of WireCast can be obtained by simply having a YouTube account (although in the past, certain parameters have been applied, such as the requirement of having a certain number of followers on your YouTube channel in order to qualify for the download). With WireCast, you have the option of streaming the video shows you produce live, or simply recording and uploading them later (which is useful if you are a podcaster who wants to offer video content, without having to stream it live every time).

Finally, if you've got a few video cameras laying around, and you're handy with programs like iMovie, there's always the option of setting up cameras in your studio and recording the show, and editing it all together later. However, depending on how much time you want to spend editing and synching the audio and video recordings afterward, as well as rendering and uploading videos (which, using this system, could take hours for a one or two-hour podcast), you may want to be careful about getting too involved with this "old-fashioned" approach to creating video renditions of your shows.

Of course, I mention this method here because, yes, I do know people who have created their video podcasts this way. But keep in mind that due to the time and work involved, some of them have also chosen to hire professional editors in order to reduce the editing and production time required later.

Going Where the Action Is: Finding Content For Your Podcast

Early on in this book, we spent a good bit of time asking questions like, "why do you want to be a podcaster?" If you've kept such questions in mind as we've progressed along, you probably are beginning to have a fairly good grasp on what the scope of your show will be, what kinds of subjects you'll address, and other details that will become integral to what your show is going to be all about.

There is more, however, to producing a podcast than just picking your favorite news sites, selecting a few stories, and reading them. Another point of equal importance for the up-and-coming podcaster is to understand that while you may not intentionally be emulating other shows in your genre, booking all the same guests that are making the rounds on those shows will do no better in helping your podcast sound different from them. You can bring all the character, pizzazz, and chutzpah to the microphone that you want, but if you are booking the same guests, and discussing the same news as other podcasters in your area of interest, then you can expect half of your show to still sound roughly the same as everyone else's podcast in your genre.

There are a number of ways to get around this. For instance, rather than going to all the same news sites most other broadcasters visit (The Drudge Report, Huffington Post, New York Times, Mother Jones, or whatever), some time ago I began using Google News to set up custom feeds based on certain subjects that interest me. This helps immensely when it comes to finding more obscure news items that often go virtually untouched, but which still cater to your interests (and of course, to the interest of your listeners).

Alternatively, let's say your podcast isn't one that focuses on news. A key piece of advice I have for any podcaster, whether or not yours is a news show, is to learn not to rely too heavily on timely material. Instead, try to find subjects that have more lasting appeal. By incorporating subjects like this into your show, you will help ensure that the replay value of that podcast episode will be greater, since it's a subject people will want to come back and listen to no matter what's happening in the world right this moment.

Another problem that emerges with finding content for your podcast is that, from time to time, a particular hot topic may arise, which several other shows will end up devoting time to. Much like the shows that all book the same guests who are making the same circles promoting their new books, your podcast can easily fall victim to the staleness of selecting subject matter that has inadvertently been worn thin already by other shows. Granted, if you have selected a *very* specific area of focus for your podcast (like, for instance, a show about lawn ornaments and varieties of garden gnomes), you may indeed find that your show is immune to this threat... *since it's the only show in the genre you've picked.* However, even if you're not in this situation, there is still hope for those who plan to hit on the hot topics of the day.

When you select a topic to discuss, yes, it's easy to pick stories and simply report the news on that subject; but one thing you may want to bear in mind is bias, and how it affects that news. Here, I'm not asking you, the podcaster, to rely on bias, thus skewing the facts favorably toward whatever it is you may be presenting. In fact, I disagree strongly with the kind of "spin" we see in most major media outlets these days. In the world of OpEds and opinion columns, we see a familiar pattern of editorializing that occurs today (not that it hasn't been this way, to some extent, for many, many decades.) The important point to bring home with you, and hope your parents will find it date-worthy, is that by virtue of being human, we're all very good at putting our own slant or "spin" on things.

So what I *am* suggesting, whether or not your show relies heavily on things like current news at all, is that you look carefully at stories or subjects, and find a unique approach to discussing them that other podcasters may not have examined.

Let's say, for example, that you've been considering doing a show on baking a particular style of bread. It's known to be a complex process, with all the mixing, and kneading, and baking, and so other shows that have addressed this process all hit on virtually the same points. How can you bring a fresh perspective to the discussion?

A few ideas might include interviewing bakeries in your area that employ experts on this particular kind of bread. Or better yet, what if you reached out to a handful of experienced bakers who *had not* ever baked this bread before, and suggested they try it as a "challenge" of some sort? Then, after their failed or successful attempts, you could interview each of them about the hurdles they faced along the way; experiential stories of "what I learned along the way" like this are popular for a reason: they help other people learn from the strengths, or failures, met by others before them.

I would invite you to consider a subject that interests you, and try brainstorming a few ways it might be covered unlike other shows have done. It may require a little more work, but if you're really trying to set yourself apart from the rest, the extra work involved will be worth it.

Be Our Guest: Booking Interviews for Your Podcast

When it comes to guests, I've already mentioned that you should attempt to avoid booking all the same guests you hear on other shows (in fact, if you're in a pinch and looking for a unique guest, before you call the professional clown down the street again and invite him on for his fourth appearance, email me instead. I'm diverse in my interests, and will happily discuss any number of subjects. Or, if we have absolutely no common ground, we'll just do what normal people do, and complain about the weather).

My opinions on booking guests stem from the way I've seen so many podcasts seek to emulate talk radio shows that are driven by an interview format. The same radio programs I'm referring to here often rely on taking open-lines calls in equal measure, but since it's more difficult for a podcaster to rely on calls from listeners, we find that the podcast genre focuses a great deal on interviews instead, simply because of their accessibility.

There's another good reason for this too, I think. Being able to listen to an interview between two people appeals to the gossip junkie in each of us. Admit it, you *love* being able to listen in on a conversation occurring somewhere nearby, and with podcast interviews, we're often treated to extended conversations to which our only commitment could be likened to that of the fly resting on the nearest wall. It's very similar in effect, just without any strings attached.

So for me, when it comes to booking interviews, I try to find a certain balance. Many of my shows have no guests, and are content-driven, where my cohosts and I will feature a discussion pertaining to a certain subject, which I feel still hits the mark in terms of presenting a sensation similar to the idea that the listener is overhearing a conversation. In fact, many great podcasts don't feature interviews with guests at all, but focus exclusively on banter that occurs between the hosts instead, a beloved form of dialogue due to the chemistry that forms between those doing the talking.

There have also been times when I come across somebody who is obviously an expert in his or her field of interest, but are otherwise unknown to the public. Sometimes, I will approach individuals like this about coming on my show. These guests actually make for some of the most interesting interviews, because they are often capable of providing both compelling content, as well as a voice entirely distinct from any that may have appeared on similar podcasts. One guest along these lines, who I reached out to and asked to come on my program, had never even been on a podcast before. Within months of appearing on my show, he had completed a book on the subject I invited him on to discuss, and was later booked on a number of other podcasts, followed by an appearance on one nationally syndicated radio program. Hey, we all have to start somewhere, right?

Which just goes to show how useful podcasts can actually be for promoting what you, and what others, are doing. Whether you bill yourself as a podcaster, or an entrepreneur who does a podcast just to help get the word out about the other things you're involved with, there are a plethora of opportunities that await anyone who is willing to promote their brand, and to take the time required to build a loyal following.

Many people think that promoting what they do requires a lot of money, but this isn't always the case. As we're about to see, there are really a lot of ways to jump-start the promotion of your podcast, and some of the most effective methods available are absolutely free.

Getting the Word Out: Promoting Your Podcast and Growing Your Audience

There are many businesses that can operate effectively with almost no advertisement, relying on word of mouth and referrals to find success. In the past, I've achieved this myself as a musician with one of my primary bands, Nitrograss, which despite having recorded no albums (yet, at least), or having any professionally produced promo videos, still manages to stay busy with work most of the year, and command good rates as well. How do we do it?

I'll tell you how: we put on a good show, and we engage our audience. As a result, at nearly every show we play, several people will come up and ask us for business cards, which direct people to our website. There, they see something that, in my opinion, is of greater importance than anything else a band can offer: *a long list of performance dates.*

Why is that important? Because our customers see the fact that we're busy year-round, and it tells them a number of things that promote confidence, such as the fact that we're willing to travel, and the fact that others are obviously willing to put their faith and dollars behind us for their events, venues, and special occasions.

I know a lot of people might think, "How could a band with no recordings find any work?" Truth is, we're primarily a cover band that features a lot of traditional music, with country, rock, and bluegrass blended into an acoustic format. This particular band, rather than being a group of artists trying to get famous and write songs destined to become timeless hits, functions as a working ensemble, which caters to events like private parties, corporate gatherings, charity operations, weddings, and other similar events. Again, it's not just about the music in our case, and in terms of being a working band, many of our friends in the region look at the prices we are able to command, and compare that with our lack of recorded material, and just can't figure it out.

The key concept I want to drive home with this example is that, rather than doing things the way most promising musicians starting out would do things, we chose instead to begin with networking by word of mouth, and were able to gain foothold starting with just a handful of shows, based on recommendations from previous contacts we had. Every show we have played since the beginning has helped us reach more people along the way, and that simple formula has continued to work to our advantage ever since.

With regard to your podcast, you're probably thinking, "okay, but how can I use word of mouth to get my podcast off the ground?" Well, there are a number of ways, but since this, unlike live performance, is primarily a digital medium, the process will be a little different.

There are four main strategies that I would first like to drive home when it comes to promoting your podcast in a grassroots way. They are as follows:

> Promote your shows by writing content-rich articles at your website's blog, and use SEO plugins to help you optimize that content

> Create a community page for your show on Facebook, where you can invite friends and others online to "Like" your page

> Create a special Twitter account for your show, and use this to engage the millions of people Twitter makes available to you

> Set up a YouTube channel associated with your podcast, and feature content that will be discovered by people searching for related subjects while surfing the web

There are other things that can be done as well, but these four are, at present, among the most effective, freely available promotional avenues for individuals creating a presence online.

Above all, you need to also remember that *search engines are your friends*. They are what will bring what you do to the world, and there is a bit of a hierarchy to how this works. When people go online to search for something, it is true that a majority of them will go to Google to look for that. According to comScore Search Engine Rankings for March 2014, "Google Sites led the U.S. explicit core search market in March with 67.5 percent market share, followed by Microsoft Sites with 18.6 percent (up 0.2 percentage points) and Yahoo Sites with 10.1 percent." AOL, once the industry leaders, marked only about 1.3 percent. In other words, things have really changed in the last few years.

"Google's dominance is multifaceted," wrote SEO specialist Jayson DeMers in *Forbes* in February 2015. "It isn't just the fact that users verbify the brand when referring to online search. It's the fact that online marketers rely almost exclusively on getting visibility through the search engine through paid advertising and SEO. And let's not forget that Google's reach extends to our email accounts, shared documents, geographic directions, news, and almost anything else you want to do online."

What Jayson was saying here is that the niche Google has carved for itself over the years has nabbed a small stake in nearly everything it's seen along the way, ranging from web searches, to emails, to funding for exotic and crazy startups like shweeb, a monorail system powered by people kicking their legs as if on a bicycle. With the wide and varied reach that Google has, you'll want to be sure that your online presence, and that of your podcast, coexist happily with Google's crawlers.

If someone goes to Google and searches for your website, it will take them to it, along with other information that may appear about it elsewhere on the web. If you have a YouTube page, any high-traffic videos you have may show up there as well; although going to YouTube and searching for your website will not, of course, bring back results for your homepage. Still, the emphasis I'm trying to make here is that both Google, and YouTube (owned by Google), work primarily as search engines. In similar fashion, iTunes, which will become the primary access point on the web for direct downloads of your show (perhaps even more than your website) also functions as a search engine; and much like YouTube videos, iTunes pages can appear in Google search results just as well.

This means that in every instance, you will want to carefully choose keywords that you can use to tag the videos you upload to YouTube, or in the description of your show on iTunes, and of course, as the keywords related to any blog post that appears at your Wordpress site. Doing so will help your show find its way to those who go searching for related subjects online. The more this happens, the more sites like YouTube and iTunes will begin to group your shows along with similar content, which leads to your program being displayed every time someone goes to look at those shows.

Many sites function in this way. Think about when you visit the product page of any item on Amazon.com. At the bottom of the page, you'll see that Amazon is more than happy to let you know that "other customers who bought this item also bought..." and so on. Making sure that what you're doing is relevant to similar content that already exists will help you greatly in the long run.

This brings us to the broader discussion about the wild and wonderful world of SEO, or **Search Engine Optimization**. There are many bloggers and podcasters I know who, while great at what they do, admit having virtually no grasp on what SEO is, or how it works. I would even argue that many probably don't even know why it's important. So let's take a minute to address that now.

Podcasting and SEO: Unmasking the Mystery

A while back, I had a good friend who wrote to me in desperation about SEO:

> Even though I'm supposed to be a seasoned blogger by now, I admit I know next to

nothing about SEO. Should I, though? Would it help increase hits on my articles? And if so, how?

Every time one of my posts gets published I try to promote the shit out of them. I plug them on Twitter, Google+ and now even on Facebook... but so far I don't really see any kind of improvement. Is there something else that could be tried?

Yes. For Wordpress sites, I strongly recommend using a plugin like the **Wordpress SEO plugin by Yoast**. This plugin will not only generate an XML sitemap for your page, but it will do things like help you make sure your page is recognized as a business or a personal page by Google. Perhaps its most helpful feature is that it allows the optimization of every page or post on a site, which incorporates a walk-through on the "Edit" page for each post that helps you allocate keywords, a title, and a host of other things. Once your page is optimized, a small, colored indicator will rank it as being red, yellow, or green, in addition to generating a checklist you can use to improve the SEO of that page or post.

Once you get the hang of using this plugin, you can actually go through, and make it a habit to ensure that every page has at least a good "green" rating for optimization. Doing this will certainly help your posts get out to the world... but since the scope of this discussion has to do with podcasts, why are we talking about writing posts on your website?

Google's crawlers work by finding content on the web... and by that, I mean *written* content. They can't scan over your podcasts and listen for keywords relevant to a subject (not yet, anyway!). But they can certainly read through a well-written summary of a podcast episode, which takes time to explain things like topics you addressed on the show, the guests you may have had, and subjects you discussed with them. You can include all kinds of information in a post that will accompany your actual podcast episode, and when it comes to optimizing your page for indexing online, the more you write, the better. Above all else, having this kind of rich information that clearly tells the web what your post is about will do a lot to help get the word out about what you do.

The inclusion of this kind of content on your podcast's website doesn't have to be limited to just summaries of posts. Some who are willing to go the extra mile actually take time to transcribe interviews with their guests, so they can be read online without having to access the podcast at all; for the podcaster, while this may sound counterintuitive, it is something that could certainly offer avenues through which content can be delivered to your site that Google's crawlers can happily index.

And of course, you can also just include articles with information about topics related to your show's subject matter, whether or not it has anything to do with a specific podcast episode. Many people tell me that they simply don't know what to write about, but generating content for a once or twice a week posting schedule actually isn't that hard. One thing you could consider is a news roundup, which features some news related to your niche, which you might put up once a week. I actually do a daily news scan (that's right, I said *daily*) which I post every morning, or occasionally outsource others to post for me. Trust me, once you get into the swing of a schedule like this, staying the course is nowhere near as daunting as it may seem at the outset, especially when you can be doing "work" like this while enjoying a cup of coffee in a Starbucks on Daytona Beach… *in January*. Whole thing takes ten minutes, no joke. Then you walk across the street, and go hang out by the beach in a salty little bar and grill. I try to do things like this from time to time, as it promotes overall happiness and clarity of thought.

Here's another idea: on your podcast, you might consider promoting something like an ongoing

Q&A, where you will field questions from your listenership by email, and then post those messages, along with your answers, on your site. In many cases, your readers and listeners will be more than happy to contribute to what you're doing in helpful ways like this, and doing so allows you to outsource ideas that are both meaningful to them, as well as low on cost for you.

Creating a Facebook Page For Your Podcast, and Whether or Not to Pay for Posts

Another great way to engage your listenership is to create a Facebook page associated with your podcast. This can be used to link to your latest episodes, as well as articles appearing on your site, and a number of other things.

Facebook also gives you access to a number of analytical tools that will help you gauge interactions with your followers, which include the posts that get the most attention. And of course, since Facebook is a social networking site, the ability to invite your friends to "Like" your page will help you reach people who will consistently see the content you are providing.

One thing I certainly like to emphasize to people is that while Facebook offers the ability to do paid for "promoted" posts, you may not find any more success with a paid promotion than you would with a well-worded description and an attention-grabbing image to accompany it. In the past, I've certainly generated a lot of interactions using paid-for posts on my Facebook pages, but the posts that have generated the *most* traffic have never been anything but regular posts I've thrown up, which had whatever those magic buzzwords are that drag people into wanting to click the link and find out more.

This is the very reason why many sensational news sites these days use article titles that fall under the category of what many call "click baiting."

Consider the following two headlines:

Man digs up old tin can filled with vintage cat photos in his back yard

Despite the strange allure we all know pictures of cats tend to have, this headline probably wouldn't have grabbed your attention like the newly "baited" rendition below might have done:

This man uncovered a strange, rusty container in his back yard. What he found inside now has people talking.

See the difference? In the latter example, it's actually what the headline *doesn't say* that grabs you. In other words, one can create an air of intrigue surrounding something that is otherwise mundane, all in the way a headline is written.

Thus, we have unraveled the mystery behind 97.8% of the media headlines we see every day.

Some sites try to maintain better standards of transparency and integrity, and hence might word the headline more like this:

Once thought lost forever, man uncovers mysterious photo collection sealed in container on his property

The story that follows is guaranteed not to be any more interesting; it's still the same old rusty coffee can, and the same ragged pictures of somebody's pet that were found inside. Notice how the inclusion of words likes "lost forever", and "uncovers" (which we used in both of the last two examples, rather than "digs up" as we saw in the first one) help lend an air of importance and urgency. Adding the term "photo collection" helps more ambiguously describe a series of pictures of somebody's cat, and "mysterious" causes the viewer to become intrigued about what the photos actually featured, without playing the "guessing game" that the click-baiting version employed.

Just as further evidence of what I'm talking about here, as I was writing this section of the book, the following *actual* headline appeared in my inbox:

'It Was a Shock': Man Finds Mysterious Box Buried in Garden of Home He's Lived in for 46 Years

Synchronicity perhaps? In this instance, rather than cat photos, the box contained the ashes of a deceased man. Still, you get the gist of the strategy I've described, and how it appears every day in the world of news headlines. I advise you employ it carefully, and don't build a reputation for overt sensationalism, lest your readers come to expect less than your alluring headlines promise in every instance, and thus choose to bypass your posts altogether.

Whether it's posts on your blog, or posts that appear on Facebook, by keeping these strategies in mind you will likely find that you can generate a lot of interest in your posts, and do so without having to pay anything. The fundamental point to remember is this: a big part of the success of what you'll do with your promotions online will involve how you choose to present them to the public.

Tweets of Fury: Using the Twitterverse to Reach the Masses

Facebook, YouTube, Wordpress, and all of the other platforms we've addressed so far are each unique in their ability to help you engage your followers. However, many in the world of self-promotion through social media would argue that Twitter just might be the best of them all.

While seemingly innocuous, and even limiting with its 140-character restriction, Twitter does employ some rather remarkable features. By the way, that character limit hails back to its early days as a primarily SMS text-driven outfit: the idea had been that limiting messages to 140-characters would allow a space of 20 characters for the username of the Tweeter, thus keeping the messages within the space of a single 160-character text message.

The result, it seems, has been an exercise in minimalism, proving once again that Shakespeare had been right when he said, "Brevity is the soul of wit." Most of us between the ages of fifteen and fifty-five are now able to keep our jokes and pickup lines well within 140 character limits, whether spoken or sent via Smartphone.

I do wonder sometimes what kinds of subversive effects—good or ill—these minimalist technologies are having on us in the broader sense. I'll have to abstain from further concern at the moment, however, since the more important focus here involves the use of the **hashtag (#)**, which you're probably already using anyway, and if you aren't, then you're probably wondering what it is.

The hashtag system on Twitter has really opened up one's ability to reach large groups of people with social media. A person with 25 or 30 followers might still be able to reach untold numbers of people by using a trending hashtag, which in turn, will likely also drive followers back to their account. Facebook's user interface is generally aimed more at helping friends find each other, and while Twitter is generally the same, many people's Twitter followers vastly outnumber their Facebook friends (even if both are within 5000, which is Facebook's friend request limit). The reason for this, in part, is because of the way Twitter's trending subject hashtag threads constantly introduce us to new people, through interest in hot topics. Facebook and other sites are still able to do this to some degree (having incorporated hashtags into their interfaces as well, for example), but not quite in the same way Twitter can.

Because of this fundamental difference, I would argue that Twitter might become one of the most useful tools in your arsenal to reach others via the web, and let them know about what you'll be doing with your podcast and related media.

As a final note on the use of social media, a great way to integrate all of these features is to use plugins with Wordpress that help get links to all of the aforementioned accounts, as well as services like Instagram, LinkedIn, Google+, and many more. You can also use Twitter and Facebook to generate widgets that you can embed on your website, so visitors to your site can "Follow" or "Like" you right from your podcast site's homepage.

Show Me the Money! Subscription Services and Using Your Podcast to Generate Income

Making money through podcasting is definitely something more and more content producers are getting involved with. While there are a host of ideas that may allow you to bring in revenue as a part of your podcasting operation, generally most of these will fall under one of the four categories we're about to address. They are as follows:

➢ Using recurring paid subscriptions

➢ Accepting donations from listeners

- Finding sponsors and selling ads

- Using your podcasts to promote a related business

I have experimented a bit with all of these various methods, and currently I offer a subscription based plan for subscribers to my Gralien Report shows, where additional content can be accessed for just $7 a month. For the most part, I have found this to be the most fruitful monetary endeavor I've tried within the scope of podcasting, although you may decide that the hassle of managing recurring payments and subscription services really just isn't your thing. Maybe you'll be great at finding sponsors for your show, on the other hand, or maybe you'll be able to appeal to the hearts and minds of your listeners well enough that they will offer support in the form of donations. I'll go over the other ways to generate revenue through podcasting in a moment, but first let's look at how subscriptions work, and why it's easier to use this method than it had been a few years ago.

If you do decide you'd like to try launching a subscription service, one of the big hurdles in the past has involved finding ways to protect your content from being accessed illegally, or having it taken by a paid subscriber and posted elsewhere online where others can gain access for free. A variety of systems have been implemented, ranging from password protected RSS feeds, to using programs and plugins that generate individual RSS feeds for every user who signs up with an account. More simply, some have used basic password protection systems where users can log in and download audio files manually from a special subscriber area on the podcaster's website; however, while I've known a few producers that have taken this route, the general consensus has been (and will no doubt remain) that people are happiest when they can have their paid podcasts sent directly to their podcatching program, the same way their free shows with an iTunes or Stitcher subscription would work.

A process for how to achieve this was described a while back, though a bit awkwardly, in the book *Podcasting for Dummies*. One the reasons I bought this book years ago had actually been because, at the time, I was interested in trying to learn new ways to make money with podcasting. Since I have mentioned this book once before, it's obvious that I've garnered a lot of good information from it, so don't get me wrong, it's full of great ideas for those new to podcasting, as well as those who have been doing it for years already. However, the portion of the book that outlines how to institute a protected

RSS feed was a bit of a letdown; it explained in a roundabout way how to implement one method of protecting an RSS feed, but in truth, the process outlined was somewhat confusing, and even though I eventually managed to implement a version of it as an experiment with one of my sites, it was far from being optimal, and left me with the impression that this was going to be much harder to do than I thought beforehand.

In defense of the authors, the truth is that the majority of podcasters out there aren't using subscription services to monetize their shows. In fact, this is *especially* the case with the majority of famous or successful people, who generally stick to things like featuring ads from sponsors on their shows. Why? The reason is simple: if somebody has a big enough name and reach that doing one podcast every week gets the job done for them (in other words, reaches a large number of listeners, and maybe even generates some income through sponsors who approach about having their ads featured on the show), then why would anybody devote their time to producing additional content on a weekly basis, and then going to the further trouble of managing all the subscriptions thereafter?

Thus, *Podcasting for Dummies*, like a number of other great books on the subject of podcasting, still manages to cover a ton of other good ideas for monetizing a podcast (and in fairness, there are also updated versions of the book that are now available; I'm referring solely to the contents in the edition I purchased around late 2013). Still, issues like this led to a lot of frustration on my part, as I deliberated on what the best way to monetize my shows might be, and whether or not I would need to hire paid professionals just to get it all to work.

Fortunately, we know that wasn't the case, thanks to the **Wishlist Member** Wordpress plugin, which I discussed in Chapter Three. This plugin, while requiring a license that starts at around $100, solved all my problems, and allowed me to easily install the plugin on my server, quickly set up the interface (which it will help walk you through), and connect it to a PayPal business account or other service of your choosing to receive payments for your subscriptions. I strongly recommend this plugin, and in fact, many podcasters I know who implement similar subscription systems either have, or are still using this plugin. You can learn all about it here: http://member.wishlistproducts.com/

Granted, there are other options you might try as well. One I had experimented with in the past was **S2Member**, which offers a comprehensive free version of their software, or the **S2Member Pro** version with additional support. However, during my time experimenting with the program, I found that I couldn't get the protected RSS function to work at all; on their support forums, I found that many other podcasters seemed to be having the same trouble, and after several weeks, and there appearing to be no resolution, I decided to try other services. Apart from this, S2Member is certainly the most cost effective, and though I didn't find it as easy to use as Wishlist Member, it isn't bad for a program that offers such a comprehensive free version.

Digital Access Pass has also emerged as one of Wishlist Member's primary competitors, offering similar services with a few different features, based on the numerous comparisons available online. Everything from their layout, to their tutorials and customer support, appears to be top of the line. Their site is http://digitalaccesspass.com/.

There are still other options available, which only shows how much things have improved in the realm of paid podcasting, especially for those who aren't professional programmers themselves. In fact, for those looking to remove themselves completely from any headaches associated with subscriber content management, companies like LibSyn are now offering services for their customers where the subscriptions are handled entirely on their end. That way, content producers only have to submit their content, and generate revenue off of it. Still, be mindful that LibSyn's model features a 50/50 profit split, which means they get half of your potential earnings, in order to have them carry out the busy work so you don't have to. For some, it may be just the ticket to incorporating a reliable, stress-free subscription service, and still generating revenue doing so.

As always, while I can make recommendations of my own all day, I always advise people do some digging before making their final decisions. So look around, and consider which methods or services are really best for what you're trying to achieve.

Donations Accepted: Reaching Out to Your Listenership With a Value-For-Value Model

With the emphasis on such things as open-source and exchange of ideas, what has become known as the **value for value** system or model is becoming increasingly popular among podcasters. This system entails the provision of content for which, if the user finds it of value, a measure of value may be returned in appreciation to the producer. In short, what that means for a podcaster is that you provide your content for free, with the understanding that your listeners may show their appreciation for the content if they find it useful by making a donation or other contribution to what you do.

Adam Curry and John Dvorak of the *No Agenda* podcast have perhaps best, and most famously, applied the value for value model to a podcasting format (I strongly advise you check them out at www.noagendashow.com). Curry, a former MTV VJ who many will remember from his days on shows like *Head Banger's Ball*, is actually important here for another reason: he was an instrumental figure in the early days of podcasting (and still is today), and is argued by many as one of the principle "fathers" of the medium, in addition to being, without question, one of it's earliest promoters. Without Curry, it's a bit hard to imagine what podcasting might have ended up being like today; and, in that true "maverick" way of getting things done, Curry and Dvorak refuse to run any advertisements on their shows, and provide all their content for free to the public, employing the value for value model to receive donations from their listeners as their sole source of funding.

The simplest way to institute a donations system for your podcast is to use PayPal. With your PayPal account, you can log in, and click "Tools" from the main dashboard. In the new window click the "PayPal Buttons" icon, and then "Create new button". Within the button creation interface, you will see a dropdown below "Choose a button type," and in it, select the type of button you wish to create (in this case, that will likely be "Donations"). Complete the rest of the form to create the button, and then copy the code you are provided and paste it someplace on your site, such as in a text widget on your Wordpress sidebar, or into the body on any other page or post.

In recent years, PayPal has tightened their policies somewhat regarding the use of their buttons for a donation system, and will advise users that if donations are received beyond a certain amount, they may be required to declare their intentions for use of the acquired funds. This has prevented some sites and blogs from using the traditional donations system, leading some to opt instead for a "Subscription" button instead, which may be set at a small donation amount that will be billed monthly, while others may have opted to go with other platforms altogether.

In the spirit of the value for value model, I am personally a fan of the idea that providing content for free can still be met with rewards, monetary or otherwise. I am equally a fan of hard work, and those willing to show support through payment; hence, in the past I have instituted different variations of the value model with some of my podcasts (in addition to donating to others who have done so as well). One thing you will certainly want to bear in mind—and this is the same whether you are charging for content outright, or if you are accepting donations on a voluntary basis—is that for people to see the value in what you do, perhaps nothing else will rank in importance above *consistency*. If you say you are going to offer the content, make sure that it is delivered, according to schedule, at least within reason. With that in mind, another thing I would offer, based on my own experience, is that you should consider whether those you may partner with will help, or hinder your effort at maintaining this consistency.

In the past, the few instances where I have experienced any failures or shortcomings with a system like value for value have always had to do with differences in opinion (and dedication) to the mutual goals I have shared with others. Once this kind of thing leads to a podcast falling out of its regular schedule, listeners will likely respond by showing less support.

So if you expect your listeners to help by supporting the content you create, remember that they will expect your consistency and reliability in equal measure. That's why they call it value for value.

Ads and Sponsorships: Selling Airtime on Your Podcast to Third Parties

For many years, the life's blood of talk radio has been its ability to generate interest among key demographics, which advertisers are willing to pay top dollar to reach with their products or services. This works with podcasting just as well, although in many cases the bigger companies who would pay for ads still prefer radio and television over podcasts, which reach a more refined niche, and thus, a smaller audience.

When it comes to the different ways to generate income through podcasting, this may be my least favorite. The reason for this, surprisingly, has nothing to do with my own background in talk radio and working alongside larger corporate entities. In fact, it's simply because bringing on sponsors means you'll have to dedicate space in your show to third parties, which in many ways can break the flow or energy of the program.

Podcast listeners, of course, love the freedom they are able to keep from loud, annoying ads one would hear on terrestrial radio. Podcast producers, on the other hand, may not always feel the same, unless what they do is truly a labor of love, and they do it more for the enjoyment of the dialogue it opens than any monetary gains they hope to derive from it. For me, it's a bit of both; I very seldom have ever sat behind a microphone and not truly enjoyed what I was doing, whether that be podcasting, or doing a live broadcast on one of my own shows, or joining as a guest on someone else's program. To do this as much as I do, one would *have* to love it, and I can honestly say that I do.

I also understand the necessity for having income, and if some of it can be generated through podcasting, that to me is a good thing.

So far as running advertisements goes, I have certainly had a number of sponsors over the years, some who have wanted as little as a banner on my website, and others who have been willing to pay more substantial amounts to get prominent placement for a live read within the podcast itself (often you'll hear these near the beginning of a show; I know at least a few big-time podcasters like Joe Rogan and Tim Ferriss will often feature sponsorship reads like this at the beginning of their podcasts).

Although most of the ads I've featured in the past have resulted from companies or individuals who contacted me, I can tell you that sitting around and twiddling your thumbs waiting for advertisers to call generally won't get you a lot of sponsorships. To really ensure that you'll land sponsorships, many podcasters I know will contact these companies themselves, and approach them with a sponsorship proposal. If sponsorships are the kind of thing you're after, you will see the most returns from reaching out to potential advertisers, and of course, it will help to be able to offer them key figures like your main demographics based on age, location, and related factors, as well as the reach (in individual downloads) that your podcast has.

There are a variety of ways you might be able to obtain this kind of information. Downloads can easily be tracked through an account with LibSyn, if you decide to go with their hosting services. You can also gather a lot of information using **Google Analytics** to monitor your site, which will help you see things like the countries and locations where your site's visitors are coming from.

It also never hurts to ask. If you want more information about your listenership, another way you can get it is to ask them for it! For instance, you could try placing a questionnaire on your website, featuring pertinent details about listening habits and other information useful for marketing purposes, and then ask them to visit your page during your show, and take a few moments to participate (make sure you give them good information on how to find it, or you might even add a link to it along with any show notes you include for your podcast's episode).

Joining Affiliate Programs and Creating Revenue Through Partnerships

Within the last few years, as many Internet giants continue to broaden the reach and scope of their operations, we have seen more and more opportunities emerge for smaller providers seeking to build partnerships with these larger entities through things like affiliate programs. While any number of companies may be willing to work out an affiliate program with you based on your podcast's subject and the number of listeners it garners, it is easier now than ever before to use affiliate ad programs with industry leaders like Google and Amazon to monetize the content you produce.

Google Adsense has become one of the most popular mediums for this available today. All you have to do is sign up and go through the account approval process, and then visit the ad toolbar and create ads, which you then place on your website. Keep in mind, however, that Google's policies state that no content promoting alcohol, tobacco, adult content, or any illegal activities may be featured on your site, and that you generally may feature no more than three ad blocks visible at the same time on any part of the site (although text link ads that they provide count separately from image banners, which is explained in their policies FAQ).

Notice, however, that these aren't ads that will actually be featured as audio within your podcast; instead these comprise banners that will appear on your podcast's website. In order for you to generate significant amounts of revenue with these, you will need to be able to drive large amounts of traffic to your site as well. Depending on whether or not you promote things like articles and other content at the site, in addition to providing a home on the web for your podcast, you may find that more people will access your show by itself through interfaces like iTunes and Stitcher, without ever visiting the site. If you decide to try Adsense, you'll need to make sure that you incorporate things that give your listeners incentive to visit your website too.

However, there is another way to incorporate **Google Ads** into your podcasting operation, especially if you're using YouTube as a medium to feature your content. With YouTube, in addition to broadening your reach beyond services like iTunes and Stitcher, you'll also have the ability to enable ads through the Video Manager area in your YouTube account. These can be configured to appear before or during your podcasts under the settings in your YouTube account, and if you build a large following, these can help generate revenue much like Google Adsense would, but using your actual shows as the medium, rather than your site.

Be mindful though, that YouTube will disable ads on any content that its algorithms recognize as being copyright protected, as we touched on earlier.

If you are a Blubrry user, CEO Todd Cochrane often mentions ways podcasters can earn money with deals Blubrry offers through national providers. This, as promoted at the Blubrry site, entails a 70/30 revenue share in favor of the podcaster, as long as a podcaster meets eligibility requirements by being Advertiser Ready, which their site will explain. You can learn all about Blubrry's program here: http://create.blubrry.com/resources/blubrry-podcast-advertising/

Another way you might consider generating revenue for your site is through the **Amazon Associates** program, which allows you to build text or image links to products on the Amazon marketplace. As an example, let's say you just interviewed an author on your show. Along with the post featuring that episode, you might link to the product detail page for their book using an Associates link, and if your listeners who heard the interview visit your site and click the link, a small kickback will be headed your way for the referral. While this, like Google Adsense, relies on your website rather than the podcast itself, I have seen many podcasters use it in this way to bring attention to products relevant to a discussion on a recent episode of their show. Hence, in the example above, the author sells a book, the podcaster gets a small cut of Amazon's sale, and the listener is able to find the book with ease, since it's linked right there on your site's page... a good deal all around.

Speaking of books, Amazon's **CreateSpace** platform allows authors to self publish books with virtually no overhead costs. In addition to books, you can print CDs and other things using this service just as well, which may be a way you can incorporate product sales into your podcast.

Or, if you want to make some customized merchandise that you can advertise on your show, such as hats and T-shirts, sites like **CafePress.com** are ready to meet your needs, featuring the ability to design and upload custom logos that can be printed onto your merchandise. They will also allow you to create an online storefront that can be integrated into your website.

Using Your Podcast to Promote Your Entrepreneurial Endeavors

Finally, of all the ways that a podcast can be used to help you increase your earnings, one of the most fun and interesting is to create a podcast that promotes your business, or something else you are involved in or passionate about.

I had a travel agent approach me a while ago with a clever idea. "What if I were to do a radio show about travel," he said. The concept was a really cool one: feature guests ranging from travelers, to journalists and authors, who made trips to interesting places around the globe, and recounted their stories and experiences. I told him I loved the idea, but that if he really wanted to maximize his potential for reaching people all over the world, and not just in his town, he would do far better taking his "radio show" idea and making it a podcast instead. Sure, most radio stations of any decent size have a built-in listenership, and hence it's true that, almost no matter what, you'll be able to pick up a number of listeners. This is still true even in smaller communities, and some of these community stations may even offer airtime for programming that can be paid for, especially on weekends. But as I've expressed throughout this book, if you're willing to explore the different ways you can combine free online services to help you build a consistent audience and expand your reach, the sky is the limit with what you can do. A podcast, in my opinion, is still the better way to go.

Generally, for almost any business owner, especially new entrepreneurs who are excited and passionate about what they do and the services they offer, I would ask you this: *why aren't you doing a podcast?* Fortunately for you, since you're reading this book, you're probably already thinking about that, if you aren't doing it already.

Now it's time to take that one step further: in other words, stop thinking, and do it. "There is no try," as Yoda told Luke Skywalker. "Only do. Do, you must."

Or as George Herbert said, "Do not wait; the time will never be 'just right.' Start where you stand, and work with whatever tools you may have at your command, and better tools will be found as you go along."

I truly love the idea behind the quote above, because it says so much about the nature of risk; whether you're an entrepreneur, or a podcaster, or one who aspires to be both, this summarizes so perfectly the necessity for getting off your laurels and doing something, no matter what the risks may be. Otherwise, you may one day look back and mourn, with the passing of time, for all the things you meant to do, but never did.

"I am an old man and have known a great many troubles, but most of them never happened." –Mark Twain

If you're passionate about what you do, you have every reason to tell the world about it. While you're at it, talk about other things you do as well, and how doing these things can improve the lives of others. It doesn't matter if that improvement is something so simple as enjoying a fresh cup of coffee, or maybe even the new coffee maker you offer through your online store that will help them make it. If you're a life coach, you can advertise your coaching services online, and tell potential clients that listen to your podcast about how you conduct sessions with Skype, like more and more consulting professionals do from home today. The possibilities are endless, and there are any number of ways you can use principles and strategies we have discussed in the pages of this book to help you bring your passion and work to a broader audience. Just get involved, and have fun with it.

After all, if you aren't having fun with what you do, then really, *what is the point of doing it?*

CHAPTER SIX: WAY OF THE MAVERICK

Quentin Tarantino isn't a guy who is known for playing by the rules. His films, as many time travelers in our audience will recognize, ignore the popular "linear" ways of storytelling in American cinema, waddling back and forth between points in time, and often making slow, seemingly-senseless emphasis on plodding conversations and weird character interactions that appear to be going nowhere. Then the next scene arrives, and violence is turned into art again, as only Tarantino really seems to know how to do.

A friend and fellow podcaster mentioned this to me recently, noting how he felt that films like *Inglourious Basterds*, whilst among his favorites, are still laboriously slow in some parts, almost relishing in their emphasis of seemingly unrelated story elements.

If you hadn't noticed already, we're doing a little of that right now, just as well. After all, what the hell do Tarantino films have to do with podcasting?

Hey, I'm no Quentin Tarantino either, but I don't have to be to tell you that he is, without question, a *maverick*. Further, I'll bet few among us, whether moviegoers, or directors themselves, would argue with me on this point. His style is defined by those elements that pair the slow, innocuous, and unusual with full-frontal visual *assaults* that create—despite the overt violence employed—beautiful and, at times, strangely haunting cinematic experiences.

Without writing a short biography about the guy, we recognize in Quentin Tarantino a nonconformist individual, and one who is uncompromising in his devotion to producing his art, and doing it *his way*.

I want you to think about that for a minute.

Many people are defined by what they achieve. However, there are many more among us who allow a fixation with how they *think* something should be achieved become the element that defines them.

Which kind are you?

Fundamental to producing something creative—whether that is a film, a book, a painting, or yes, a podcast—is finding your own special voice. Sure, I couldn't spend time writing a book for you about podcasting if I didn't examine a lot of the technical aspects about it first. Here, the equipment we've covered, and the methods for their use, are the brushes, paints and palettes of the audio-artist; but more is required before what you make when you sit down behind a microphone can truly be called "art."

Then again, some might ask whether a podcast can really be called "art" in the first place. I think so, although I see more and more these days that the podcasting medium has become other things too: apart from purely being a form of entertainment, for some of us, it has become a tool that utilizes information in an audio format for the purpose of branding the work of the podcaster. There is absolutely nothing wrong with this, of course; I'm not saying I think that every person who sits down behind a microphone should be producing stellar instances of "theatre of the mind" in every session, and in truth, doing so would require far more than most have the time, or the technical skills, to achieve.

On the other hand, there is a beauty to be found in the Spartan simplicity of a show that utilizes very little in the way of colorful sounds and mixes, emphasizing instead the discussion between hosts and guests to still succeed at creating a "colorful" podcasting experience. While I prefer having music, sound effects, and similar elements incorporated into my shows, and often in very elaborate ways, I don't think that these things are necessary in all cases. In truth, there is only one element that really must exist for it to qualify as being a podcast: that, as we have established already, is the human voice.

So whether you're a Tarantino who uses the slow silence between plot points to accentuate the peaks that will follow; or perhaps a Hitchcock who builds suspense carefully along the way; or maybe a George Lucas, who combines the best elements of spaghetti westerns with science fiction, creates some of the greatest fantasy films of our time, and then curiously seeks to wreck them with ponderous CGI effects added in several decades later, you can see that there are any number of ways art can be achieved. It is a different process, and a different vision, for each who seeks to create it; this beauty of individuality is the key to mastering the "art" of the podcast, as well.

Podcasting Isn't Just Art: It's a Tool That Can Help You Achieve Freedom and Individuality

One of the most interesting things about podcasting to me has always been the idea that you can take what you do with you virtually anywhere you go. Whether you do podcasts just for fun, or as a way to promote your brand, or as part of a paid-for service which you actually monetize, it's one of those unique aspects of what you do that you can take along for the ride.

This is of great importance, because when this fundamental realization is made, one can also begin to see that podcasting, and the kinds of business endeavors that work well with it, presents you with unique opportunities that fall into the category of *lifestyle shaping*.

What do I mean by "lifestyle shaping"? It means precisely what it sounds like: taking control of how you live, and what you do, and building the kind of life you want to have, rather than the one you feel obligated to lead.

The Internet has broadened the way we interact with the world, and with each other. By doing so, it has also helped remove a lot of the previous restrictions that once existed in terms of jobs, the workplace, and mobility. More and more people are able to work from home, or even take their work with them wherever else they may go.

A few years ago, when I was still working in the radio business, I began to see what I felt were problems with the way our business was modeled. This was due, in part, to a general decline in interest in radio that was occurring at that time; as more people were being added to our sales team, who worked on a commission basis to get out there and fight over what little could be found in the way of new advertisers, the programming and production staff (which I was part of) kept being trimmed back further, causing fewer people to have to carry all the work of the full staff we couldn't afford any longer. None of the trimming, or the increased sales presence, was matching the new competition that had entered the market: things like satellite radio, iPods with customizable playlists of music people actually *liked* hearing, and of course, the rise in interest occurring at that time in a new medium called podcasting.

Despite the skeleton crew we maintained over on the creative end of things, I consistently found that in my department, the work before me could easily have been undertaken and completed in roughly half the time I was required to actually remain in my office. Thus, I spent the remainder of my full-time hours trying to find other things to do: "busy work", in other words, which seemed wasteful to say the least.

After considering my situation, I thought it might help if I offered to work on a part-time basis instead. Not only was I confident that going part time would provide enough hours to fulfill my obligations, but I also realized that the majority of my voiceover and production work could easily be done from home, allowing me to work on other things like writing and blogging, which I had begun to pursue heavily in my spare time. So I approached my supervisor, and made my big proposal: if I trimmed back my hours, this would help save the company time and money, and it would free me up to pursue my other interests without compromising our workflow, or losing my job entirely. It seemed, to me, like a winning proposition for both parties.

My supervisor, a good friend of mine, just didn't agree with the idea. "This department requires a full time assistant," he said.

Sure, I understood where he was coming from, but here I was, stuck making introductory wages in radio, and without enough work to justify the hours I was required to spend in the studio. Furthermore, I guessed at the time that, at around the age of 25, I was one of the youngest full time employees in the entire market. Hence, without age or tenure on the job—"seat time", as my boss called it—I was sure I was probably drawing the smallest paychecks of anyone on staff, just as well.

My next strategy was to ask for a raise, and perhaps for more work as well, but that idea fell flat too. "I did what I could," my supervisor told me after a visit to the office of our business manager, "but there just isn't any budget for raising your salary right now."

So, with a heavy heart, I decided to quit.

For me, there were no harsh feelings, and I felt no other dissatisfaction, apart from my fundamental philosophy about things: I perceived the situation as one where my supervisors felt they were doing some kind of "favor" for me by keeping me full-time, when in fact, on my end of things, it seemed like it was a big waste of time—mine and theirs—and without any significant benefit to either party.

Lately, I feel that more and more people have begun to find themselves in situations similar to this, especially with the way the Internet is changing what can, or what even *has* to be done, in the office. A couple of examples:

➢ As more positions in the workplace involve work on computers that can be accessed from anywhere online, the requirement of having to remain in the office is reduced

➢ Many people who are laid off from their jobs, rather than looking for new work, begin to look at web-based opportunities for self employment, like creating products and services marketed online

➢ Some people with entrepreneurial endeavors they manage on the side find their pet projects are taking off, thanks in part to the reach of the web, and they quit their day jobs to pursue these projects full time

I want to very respectfully acknowledge that not everyone may have an entrepreneurial endeavor they are running on the side, or some other skill that they feel they could fall back on if they were to lose their job. And of course, quitting just because you don't like your job, or aspects of it, may not be the right move either. I don't want to try and make it sound like quitting your day job and striking out on your own is "easy", or that it's something that just anybody can do. You aren't going to just launch into podcasting, for instance, and use it as a magical gateway to finding your new calling overnight. In fact, there is inevitably going to be a lot of work involved, and anyone who tells you that striking out on your own is an easy, risk-free thing to do just isn't being honest. Conversely, becoming a podcaster—and a really great one—doesn't require being self-employed, or making money from doing it. For some, podcasting may just be the fun pastime you'll enjoy on the weekends, and that's fine too.

So in the context of this discussion about the philosophy of living and finding your own path, I do want to emphasize that podcasting is not only something that many of you will enjoy doing, but it may also help you along the way. It is a medium that can serve as a promotional avenue for other things you do, and it is just as flexible as self-employment can be, especially once you've found success with it.

For me, since working in radio was the job I was walking away from, and since podcasting was something I wished to do more of, it was a no-brainer. I could sit in front of a microphone for eight hours a day, five days a week, making a meager income, or I could go into business for myself, keep doing work with podcasting that was similar to what I did (and enjoyed) in radio, and do it all on my own time, from virtually anywhere I might go.

The "maverick" mindset that I'm expressing to you here is one of finding your own unique path. It is not an "easy escape" from the everyday; it means taking the road less traveled, which is often anything but easy. With time, and persistence, applying it to your various projects and endeavors may grant you freedom and flexibility that no typical "day job" would offer, but only if you put in the time and trouble required to reach the future goal of independence.

Podcasting, I feel, really is something that can help you with this. It's also a lot of fun, and a great way to broaden your available resources, as well as expand your horizons.

Above All Else...

With this book, we have spent a lot of time here together looking at the tools and techniques that form the art of podcasting, and the various ways this medium can be used to help you reach other goals you may have in life.

With our discussion about the philosophy of living, freedom, and the hard work that goes into achieving such things, at the moment I'm reminded of a rather odd quote, which American author Hunter S. Thompson (yes, also a maverick) included in his book *Fear and Loathing on the Campaign Trail '72*. Thompson came across the quote in a copy of *California Living* Magazine, and included it near the end of his book, just as I plan to do here as we are nearing the end of mine.

It read as follows:

"Press on. Nothing in the world can take the place of persistence. Talent will not: nothing is more common than unsuccessful men with talent. Genius will not: unrewarded genius is almost a proverb. Education alone will not: the world is full of educated derelicts. Persistence and determination alone are omnipotent."

I've always found that passage a little odd—maybe it had been the context in which Thompson used it—but hopefully you also see why I included it here. It is actually attributed to Calvin Coolidge, and it has always stuck in my mind for the wisdom it carries.

To succeed at anything requires persistence, and a fair degree of determination as well. I've enjoyed listening to many podcasters over the years who didn't have very "trained" or professional sounding voices, and others who may not have had the deepest perspectives on things going on in the world. But some of them knew how to ask great questions of the guests they invited onto their shows, and how to do things so simple as having a good conversation. They learned, with time, the simple formulas that helped make a podcast fun and exciting to listen to. These were individuals that learned all they could about the medium, and then worked hard at making it their own, rather than making it into something that somebody else taught them it should be.

Of greater importance, they made sure that whatever they did, they never lost themselves, and remained true to their own ideals as they went on to succeed with their goals.

To any podcaster, I say make what you are doing fun, and make sure you do it often. *Make it your* own. Be creative, and try to communicate and share ideas with others, whether they are fellow podcasters, or merely those among the crowd who listen and enjoy them.

We are living the *greatest* adventure right now: it is the amazing journey of life. With podcasting, the audio recordings you make will not only provide entertainment and information for others; they will capture moments and memories for you along that personal journey that each of us makes. From time to time, you may happen upon them again in years to come, and recognize them as having been stones along the path that helped to guide you: the proverbial breadcrumbs that lead us home by the moonlight.

Rather than worrying about what may come, I only ask that you always look to the road ahead of you with appreciation, and with an attitude of grace, persistence, and gratefulness for the adventure that awaits.

Don't focus too heavily on where you're going, or how you're going to get there. Let each day come, and go where the path may lead.

And above all else, *enjoy the ride.*

APPENDIX: PODCASTING RESOURCES

As a final added bonus with this book, I wanted to include a few resources for you that can be quickly referenced here in this appendix, which include a reading list of books by other podcasting professionals, as well as various websites with tutorials, information, music for use in podcasts, legal information, and even articles that seek to make sense of the explosive popularity we're seeing with podcasting today. It is my hope that these resources may prove useful, along with the broader concepts we've spent time covering in this book.

Speaking of books, first let's take a look at my recommended reading list.

Books on Podcasting

There are many, *many* titles dealing with the subject of podcasting, several of which are available through mediums like Kindle for just pennies on the dollar. This list covers a few of the most popular books on the subject, as well as a few I have personally found helpful as a podcaster who, like many, has questions from time to time. In addition to these, I also highly recommend you visit a site like Amazon.com and simply do a keyword search for the term "podcasting", where you'll no doubt find other titles that may be helpful for you, which there simply isn't space to include here.

Sound Reporting: The NPR Guide to Audio Journalism and Production by Jonathan Kern.

Whether or not you are a fan of National Public Radio (though many of us are), this book will give you a unique insight into audio production from the perspective of broadcast journalists, and how it is best applied when approaching news and current events. In many ways, what they offer contrasts greatly with the approach I present in this guide, and Kern gives a more procedural, "by the book" approach, rather than the DIY wizardry we have examined here. This, in essence, is precisely why I've listed it first among my recommended reading for aspiring podcasters.

Podcastnomics: The Book Of Podcasting... To Make You Millions by Naresh Vissa.

Arguably one of the most attractive books on the subject in the last few years, this bestseller on the subject, "touted as one of the great primers on podcasting," looks at everything from how to set up your gear and create a podcasting empire, to marketing your shows for profit. Those hoping to make money with their podcasting endeavors may find this book an invaluable addition to their collection.

Podcast Solutions: The Complete Guide to Audio and Video Podcasting, 2nd Edition by Michael W. Geoghegan and Dan Klass.

This is another book that covers podcasting in a very meticulous fashion, looking at all aspects of the art. As I've outlined for you in this guide, there are some aspects of podcasting on the more technical side of things that you may not need to become an expert in just to be able to produce podcasts on par with other professionals. However, a book like this is a valuable resource to have in general, as well as a great place to get ideas and advice if you ever do decide to delve into more technical aspects of podcasting.

Podcasting For Dummies, 2nd Edition by Tee Morris, Chuck Tomasi, and Evo Terra.

This book is a standard that, like Geoghegan and Klass's book above, I recommend podcasters have a copy of, if for nothing else but the value it offers as a reference on the subject. Virtually all aspects of podcasting are covered, and I have managed to learn a number of things, in addition to finding inspiration for new ideas of my own, from things they cover in it. The authors also contributed to a second volume, **Expert Podcasting Practices For Dummies**, which as the name implies, goes a bit further beyond the offerings covered in their initial book on the subject.

How To Podcast 2015: Four Simple Steps To Broadcast Your Message To The Entire Connected Planet - Even If You Don't Know Where To Start by Paul Colligan.

While covering most of the same sorts of concepts we've looked at in this book, Paul Colligan offers an up-to-date perspective on podcasting, and how the absolute beginner can launch into it with or without any experience in audio recording or other related fields.

Niche Podcast Profits: How To Turn Your Passion To Profits With Podcasting by Jason Jerzewski.

I've included this book because it offers some valuable perspectives on podcasting from a marketing standpoint, with specific interest in using a podcast to promote a niche business endeavor. This, in essence, is the same concept that I cover in the final chapters of this book, where I discuss using a podcast specifically to promote a business interest or passion. In the world of niche marketing, using podcasts to promote what you do is becoming one of the leading avenues for reaching more people. For more information on niche pursuits, I also recommend looking at Spencer Hawes website, www.nichepursuits.com, along with Pat Flynn's site, www.smartpassiveincome.com. Each of these will provide you with invaluable information on how to find a niche worth pursuing in the first place, and what you can do to grow that idea into a profitable business online.

Websites, Resources and Tutorials

Here, I've created a list of excellent websites about podcasting, editing, and recording audio on a budget, as well as a few pages on sites dealing with other content with information beneficial to podcasters. If you haven't already, I highly recommend that you check out some of these resources.

Cliff Ravenscraft, The Podcast Answer Man: http://podcastanswerman.com/

Ray Ortega's The Podcaster's Studio: http://thepodcastersstudio.com/

Dave Jackson's School of Podcasting:
http://schoolofpodcasting.com/

Pat Flynn's excellent tutorial (with videos) on "How to Start a Podcast":
http://www.smartpassiveincome.com/how-to-start-a-podcast-podcasting-tutorial/

Auphonic.com's tutorial on "How to Podcast for Free": https://auphonic.com/blog/2013/02/07/how-to-podcast-for-free/

Ryan Pierson's article on "Podcasting On A Budget: How To Record Great Audio For Less":
http://readwrite.com/2015/05/02/audio-podcasting-on-a-budget

The Complete Guide to Creating and Editing Podcasts with Audacity
http://www.technorms.com/29516/how-to-create-and-edit-podcasts-audacity

The Wordpress Codex: an online resource for all things Wordpress:
http://codex.wordpress.org/Main_Page

The Creative Commons Corporation Podcasting Legal Guide:
https://wiki.creativecommons.org/wiki/Podcasting_Legal_Guide

Sites for Finding Music for Podcasts

Here are just a few sites, in addition to common resources like YouTube, where podcasters can access music for use in podcasts. Keep in mind that some of these resources may require licensing, attribution, one-time fees, or other arrangements in conjunction with the use of the services provided:

Music for Podcasts from Royalty Free Music: www.royaltyfreemusic.com

Free Music Archive: www.freemusicarchive.org

Stock Music Online: www.stockmusic.net

Internet Archive's Online Community Audio Project:
http://www.archive.org/details/opensource_audio

"New Music Podcast" Music Library by Beatsuite.com (available through iTunes):

https://itunes.apple.com/us/podcast/royalty-free-music-new-music/id191712529?mt=2

Online Articles About Podcasting

These articles deal with things that include important data pertaining to podcasts, trends, and other things relative to the growing industry that surrounds podcasts. Although they aren't "how-to" resources, I list them because they discuss some of the cultural impact podcasts are having in relation to things like "New Media" and entertainment.

"Podcasting Fact Sheet" by Nancy Vogt, based on data from the Pew Research Center (updated April, 2015):
http://www.journalism.org/2015/04/29/podcasting-fact-sheet/

New York Magazine explores "What's Behind the Great Podcast Renaissance?":
http://nymag.com/daily/intelligencer/2014/10/whats-behind-the-great-podcast-renaissance.html

Rebecca Greenfield looks at "The (Surprisingly Profitable) Rise of Podcast Networks" in *Fast Company*:
http://www.fastcompany.com/3035954/most-

creative-people/the-surprisingly-profitable-rise-of-podcast-networks

"The Voices: Toward a critical theory of podcasting." Jonah Weiner writes for *Slate* about why we find podcasts so addicting and pleasurable: http://www.slate.com/articles/arts/ten_years_in_you r_ears/2014/12/what_makes_podcasts_so_addictive _and_pleasurable.html

For More on Maverick Podcasting

Finally, you will be able to find more information about this book, as well as updates on my continuing adventures in maverick podcasting, at the following websites:

www.micahhanks.com
www.maverickpodcasting.org

INDEX

C

D

R

S

ABOUT THE AUTHOR

Micah Hanks is a writer, podcaster, and researcher whose interests include history, science, current events, cultural studies, technology, business, philosophy, unexplained phenomena, and ways the future of humankind may be influenced by science and innovation in the coming decades. With his writing, he has covered topics that include controversial themes such as artificial intelligence, government surveillance, unconventional aviation technologies, and the broadening of human knowledge through the reach of the Internet.

Micah lives in the heart of Appalachia near Asheville, North Carolina, where he makes a living as a writer and musician.

SEP 2 9 2016